Wild & Witty CAKES

Greg & Max

MEREHURST

This book is dedicated to Aris Ttoffalli, a friend, a good man and a fine human being.

Published 1994 by Merehurst Limited, Ferry House, 51–57 Lacy Road, Putney, London SW15 1PR

Text Copyright © Greg Robinson and Max Schofield 1994
Photography and design Copyright © Merehurst Limited 1994

ISBN 1 85391 324 3

A catalogue record of this book is available from the British Library.

Edited by Helen Southall
Designed by Anita Ruddell
Photography by Clive Streeter

Colour separation by P & W Graphics, Singapore
Printed in Italy by Milanostompa SpA

Cook's Notes

For all recipes, quantities are given in metric, Imperial and cup measurements. Follow one set of measures only as they are not interchangeable. Standard 5ml teaspoons and 15ml tablespoons are used. Australian readers, whose tablespoons measure 20ml, should adjust quantities accordingly. All spoon measures are assumed to be level unless otherwise stated. Eggs are a standard size 3 (medium) unless otherwise stated.

Contents

Introduction

Welcome to the wonderful world of *Wild and Witty Cakes*, a fun-filled phantasmagoria of fabulous frivolity. Phew!

These light-hearted, tongue-in-cheek designs depict everyday objects and scenes, which, as you will see, have been given a bit of a twist! In this way, a cup of cappuccino becomes the bearer of a romantic message, and even a cactus can raise a naughty smile. One of the best things about the cakes in this book is that simply by changing their message, they can be adapted to suit any occasion or celebration. Feel free to change any of the colours or details if your occasion demands a slightly different cake. After all, this book is just a starting point – as well as allowing you to copy our designs faithfully, we hope it will stimulate loads of your own ideas.

We have had great fun writing this book and making the cakes – now it's over to you.

Greg + Max.

Basic Techniques

This first chapter is not here just to fill space by trotting out the same old information. On the contrary, we hope it contains some nuggets of good sense, pearls of wisdom and tips and time-savers galore, all based on years of experience and more than a few mistakes along the way – like the time we iced a cake and left it on the work surface expecting to be able to move it on to a cake board the next day, only to find it stuck solid; or the time we assumed that marzipan and icing would somehow defy the laws of gravity only to watch an elaborate cake decoration fall off in slow motion before our very eyes; or the time we thought we could deliver a three-tier American-style wedding cake covered in Italian meringue to a reception by taxi, only to find ourselves up to the wrists in meringue at the end of a road containing seven speed humps, and with a taxi driver who thought he was Nigel Mansell!

We can't emphasize enough just how important it is to read and follow instructions carefully, both in this section and in the cake designs that follow. So, take a few minutes to save yourself making your own mistakes before you plunge headlong into the wonderful world of *Wild and Witty Cakes*.

Cake Recipes

RICH FRUIT CAKE

This cake produces a wonderfully fruity cake that is not too dark. See the chart on page 9 for ingredients, quantities, oven temperature and baking times.

1 Line the required cake tin with a double thickness of greaseproof or non-stick paper, and wrap a double thickness of brown paper around the outside of the tin, securing it with string. Put the dried fruit, half the flour, the spices, glacé cherries, ground almonds and peel into a clean polythene bag. Hold the neck of the bag closed and shake the ingredients so that the fruit is coated in flour.

2 Put the butter or margarine in a bowl with the sugar, and cream together. Beat in the eggs, one at a time, each followed by a spoonful of the remaining flour. When all the eggs and flour have been added, tip the dried fruit mixture into the bowl and stir. Turn the mixture into the prepared tin, level the surface, and bake in the oven for the time given in the chart.

3 Rich fruit cakes take a long time to cook; to prevent the top of the cake becoming too brown, put a double thickness of brown paper over the cake halfway through cooking. At this point, you might also reduce the cooking temperature to 140°C (275°F/Gas 1) until the cake is cooked. To test whether the cake is ready, insert a fine skewer or cocktail stick into the centre. If the cake is cooked, it will come out clean. If any cake mixture adheres to the skewer, put the cake back in the oven. When you are happy the cake is cooked, remove it from the oven and leave it to cool in the tin.

4 Turn the cake out of the tin and peel off the lining paper. Wrap the cake in greaseproof or non-stick paper until required.

5 If you like, you can 'feed' the cake with alcohol before wrapping it. Turn the cake upside down and prick it all over with a cocktail stick. Spoon the alcohol of your choice (brandy, sherry or rum) liberally over the cake – don't stint, the cake will not taste overwhelmingly of alcohol, but wonderfully mature. You can 'feed' the cake like this several times.

MADEIRA SPONGE CAKE

See the chart on page 9 for ingredients, quantities, oven temperature and baking times.

1 Grease the required tin and line it with greaseproof or non-stick paper.

2 Cream the butter or margarine and sugar together in a bowl until light and fluffy, and pale in colour. Beat in the eggs, one at a time, following each one with a spoonful of the flour. Sift the remaining dry ingredients together and fold them into the creamed mixture followed by the lemon juice. Turn the mixture into the prepared tin, level the surface and bake in the oven for the time given in the chart or until well risen, firm to the touch and golden brown.

3 Allow the cake to cool in the tin for 5–10 minutes, then turn out on to a wire rack. Remove the lining paper and leave the cake to cool completely.

Cook's tip

Remember that the cooking times given for the cakes are only approximate. Oven temperatures do vary enormously; if your oven is fan-assisted, for example, you might need to reduce the stated temperatures according to your oven manufacturer's handbook. A general rule of thumb is that when you can smell the cake cooking, it is nearly ready. However, the fingertip-test is more accurate for sponge cakes – if the cake is firm to the touch, it is ready.

MADEIRA SPONGE CAKE

	ROUND				SQUARE	
	15cm (6 inch)	20cm (8 inch)	25cm (10 inch)	30cm (12 inch)	25cm (10 inch)	30cm (12 inch)
Butter or margarine, softened	185g (6oz)	250g (8oz)	315g (10oz)	500g (1lb)	500g (1lb)	750g (1½lb)
Caster sugar	185g (6oz/ ¾ cup)	250g (8oz/1¼ cups)	315g (10oz/1½ cups)	500g (1lb/2½ cups)	500g (1lb/2½ cups)	750g (1½lb/3¾ cups)
Eggs	3	4	5	8	8	12
Self-raising flour	185g (6oz/1½ cups)	250g (8oz/2 cups)	315g (10oz/2½ cups)	500g (1lb/4 cups)	500g (1lb/4 cups)	750g (1½lb/6 cups)
Plain flour	90g (3oz/ ¾ cup)	125g (4oz/1 cup)	155g (5oz/1¼ cups)	250g (8oz/2 cups)	250g (8oz/2 cups)	375g (12oz/3 cups)
Lemon juice	1 tbsp	1½ tbsp	2 tbsp	3 tbsp	3 tbsp	5 tbsp
Baking time (approx.)	1¼ hours	1¼ –1½ hours	1½ hours	1½–1¾ hours	1½–1¾ hours	2–2¼ hours
Oven temperature	160°C (325°F/Gas 3)					

RICH FRUIT CAKE

	ROUND				SQUARE	
	15cm (6 inch)	20cm (8 inch)	25cm (10 inch)	30cm (12 inch)	25cm (10 inch)	30cm (12 inch)
Mixed dried fruit	315g (10oz)	655g (1 lb 5oz)	1.18kg (2lb 6oz)	4.12kg (4¼ lb)	1.7kg (3lb 6oz)	2.62kg (5¼lb)
Plain flour	125g (4oz/1 cup)	250g (8oz/2cups)	440g (14oz/3½ cups)	750g (1½lb/6 cups)	655g (1lb 5oz/5¼ cups)	875g (1lb 13oz/7 ¼ cups)
Ground mixed spice	¼ tsp	½ tsp	1 tsp	1½ tsp	1¼ tsp	1¾ tsp
Ground cinnamon	½ tsp	¾ tsp	1½ tsp	2½ tsp	2 tsp	2 ¾ tsp
Glacé cherries	60g (2oz)	125g (4oz)	185g (6oz)	315g (10oz)	250g (8oz)	375g (12oz)
Ground almonds	30g (1oz/¼ cup)	60g (2oz/½ cup)	125g (4oz/1¼ cups)	220g (7oz/2 cups)	155g (5oz/1⅓ cups)	280g (9oz/2½ cups)
Chopped mixed peel	30g (1oz)	60g (2oz)	125g (4oz)	220g (7oz)	155g (5oz)	280g (9oz)
Butter or margarine, softened	125g (4oz)	185g (6oz)	375g (12oz)	655g (1lb 5oz)	560g (1lb 2oz)	875g (1¾ lb)
Soft brown sugar	125g (4oz/¾ cup)	185g (6oz/1 cup)	375g (12oz/2 cups)	655g (1lb 5oz/4 cups)	560g (1lb 2oz/3⅓ cups)	875g (1¾ lb/5 cups)
Eggs	2	3	6	11	9	14
Baking time (approx.)	2 hours	2¾ hours	3¾ hours	5¼ hours	4½ hours	6 hours
Oven temperature	150°C (300°F/Gas 2)					

Making Templates

For some of the cakes in this book, you will need to make a template, either to help create the basic shape of the cake or to cut out decorative shapes from icing. All the shapes, designs and outlines you need are given, but in some cases the design has been reduced in size in order to fit into the format of the book. However, increasing the size of a design is quite straightforward. To make a template, trace the required design on to greaseproof or non-stick paper.

To transfer the design to thin card, as for the Tartan Christmas cake (see page 79) for example, place a piece of carbon or graphite paper between the greaseproof sheet and the card, and go over the design again. (Graphite paper is like carbon paper except that the outline it leaves contains traces of lead. Graphite can also be used to transfer a design on to icing, but, because of the lead, it is best to use this only on decorative pieces of icing that you do not intend to eat.) Cut out the card around the design.

If you need to increase or decrease the size of the traced design, one option is to take it to a photocopy or print shop where it will be possible to have a copy made to whatever size you wish, and at very little cost. However, if you do not have a print shop close by, then you can make a copy yourself. Draw a square around the design to fit as tightly as possible. Divide each side of the square into five equal parts, and then join up the marks from top to bottom and side to side, giving you 25 smaller squares. Now draw a square on another piece of paper that will just contain the design enlarged to the size you want it. Divide this larger square into 25 smaller squares as above. Copy the design from the smaller to the larger grid, square by square. Although you are drawing freehand, the squares will guide you.

Some cakes require an outline or written message to be transferred on to a fondant-iced surface. This is achieved by tracing the outline on to greaseproof or non-stick paper, laying it over the icing, and then gently going over it again, using the end of a cocktail stick, paintbrush, pencil, or something similar, pressing hard enough to leave an impression in the icing. It is a good idea to let the icing firm up slightly for 2–3 hours before transferring an outline or message on to it, otherwise you will find that even the slightest pressure of fingertips or the heel of your hand holding the paper in position, will leave an indentation that you don't want. Once the icing has hardened, the outline can be painted with whatever colour of food colouring you like.

To transfer a message on to a hardened piece of gelatin or fondant icing that you do not intend to eat, trace the message on to greaseproof or non-stick paper and use carbon or graphite paper to transfer it to the icing.

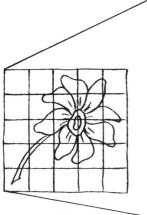

The quickest, simplest (and laziest!) way to enlarge a traced outline is to take it to your local print shop where you can have it photocopied to whatever size you want.

To enlarge a design, copy it one square at a time from the smaller grid to the larger one. It couldn't be simpler!

Carving

Some of the cakes in this book feature the technique of carving, either to create a simple design, such as Cactus Willy (see page 24) or something slightly more complicated such as Frog Prince (see page 53). The important thing to remember when you intend carving cake is that the actual cake itself should be able to withstand the process.

The cake designs featured in this book are made from either Madeira sponge or rich fruit cakes, both of which are perfect for carving because they are firm and close-textured. Some other types of cake are not suitable for carving – a whisked Génoise sponge, for example, is too light and full of air; if you were to stack these cakes one on top of the other, the air would be forced out, and the cake would sink. It would sink even further when marzipan and icing were added. Moreover, very light whisked Génoise and Victoria sponges tend to 'snag' when you try to carve them, so the cake falls into chunks rather than being carved in neat slices. Cakes that are made using oil instead of margarine or butter, as in some carrot cakes, for example, are not suitable because the increased moisture and density makes them difficult to work with. Before you start, therefore, always consider whether the cake you have baked will be able to withstand the process you have in mind for it.

In this book, we have used Madeira sponges in the photographs to illustrate carving techniques. In order to make the photographs as clear and easy to follow as possible, we did not put fillings in the cakes illustrated, but you will obviously want to include a delicious filling in your cakes. For carving purposes, however, there are a couple of points worth bearing in mind. Firstly, squidgy layers of cream and jam are lovely in a cake at teatime, but are a nightmare in a cake that you intend carving. If the filling is too thick and soft, it will ooze out when you apply the necessary pressure for carving. This is not only messy but it also means that the lines you carve will change as the filling oozes out. It is essential, therefore, to avoid fresh cream as a filling and that buttercream fillings are exactly that, i.e. made from butter! Remember that one of the characteristics of some margarines is that they spread easily straight from the fridge. This also means that they stay soft out of the fridge – and squidgy to boot. If you include jam, don't be too heavy-handed with the jam, otherwise the layers of the cake will slide around, making carving very difficult. Simply fill the cake with layers of buttercream (see the recipe on page 15) and jam, and leave it for 1–2 hours to firm up.

Most cakes rise unevenly during cooking. We usually cut off the resulting 'dome' to make a regular block of cake. Collect these offcuts together with the other pieces of cake you carve off, and they can be used to make desserts, such as trifles, baked alaskas and truffles (see

Although delicious, a thick filling of whipped cream and jam is not recommended for a cake that is to be carved.

11

recipe right). Even fruit cake can be used in the bottom of an 'adult' trifle, or added to ice cream to make a kind of cassata.

Don't worry about special equipment for carving – ordinary household knives are fine, although bendy blades are a bit awkward and best avoided. Knives don't need to be razor sharp, but avoid using one with a blunt blade. A knife with a serrated edge is useful for fruit cakes. A long-bladed knife is good for making large cuts, while a smaller one helps with the finer detail.

Trifle and truffles made from leftover pieces of sponge or fruit cake are delicious!

A SIMPLE TRUFFLE RECIPE

Put all Madeira cake offcuts (including any buttercream and jam filling) into a food processor. Blend until smooth, then add some cocoa powder (to taste), and blend again. Turn into a bowl and put in the fridge to firm up. When firm enough to handle, take a teaspoonful at a time and roll it in your hands to make balls. If the crumbs refuse to stick together, add a little more jam. To finish, roll in chocolate vermicelli and store in foil cases. Keep cool until you want to eat them. Surprisingly delicious!

Icing Recipes

On the whole, we have used two basic types of icing throughout this book – fondant and gelatin. Fondant or ready-to-roll icing can be bought ready-made in shops and supermarkets, but we have included a recipe so you can try making your own. In our experience, some commercial brands are very sweet and smell very synthetic. However, on the positive side, they can be bought ready-coloured, which means you don't have to worry about getting the colour right. The choice is yours.

FONDANT ICING

Fondant icing produces a soft, moulded finish that is easy to cut and does not splinter like royal icing. It is quick and easy to use after a little practice. If the icing feels a little dry, or fine cracks appear when rolling it out, simply add a few drops of water and knead again until soft and pliable.

Makes 500g (1lb)

500g (1lb/3 cups) icing sugar
1 large egg white
30ml (6tsp) liquid glucose
icing sugar for dusting

1 Put the icing sugar, egg white and liquid glucose in a bowl and mix with a wooden spoon until the mixture looks like lumps of breadcrumbs. At this point it is best to continue mixing by hand, adding a little extra icing sugar if the mixture seems sticky.

2 Knead the icing until it leaves the sides of the bowl clean and does not stick to your hands. It should be possible to roll out the icing on a work sur-face lightly dusted with icing sugar without it sticking. Just as when you are rolling out pastry, be sure to keep sprinkling icing sugar on the work surface as you roll out the icing.

3 Once you have made your fondant icing, wrap it tightly in plastic food wrap. It can be used straight away, but we find that if you leave it for several hours you get fewer air bubbles in the icing when you roll it out. If you do find air bubbles in the icing, simply push a fine needle at an angle into each bubble to release the air. Gently rub over the hole with your fingertip and it should close up.

ROYAL ICING

This is used in the making of some icing flowers, and to stick decorations to some cakes. You can buy instant royal icing, but if you prefer to make your own, here is a recipe.

Makes 375g (12oz/1½ cups)

1 large egg white
375g (12oz/2¼ cups) icing sugar

Beat the egg white to break it up, and add the icing sugar in batches, mixing after each addition. Add sufficient icing sugar to reach the required consistency for what you have in mind. For example, in I Knew You Were Coming So I Baked A Cake (see page 83), the icing needs to be firm but spreadable, while it needs to be quite stiff if you are using it to stick things on to a cake.

13

Cook's tip

Some people get terribly anxious about, for example, exactly how much 1 teaspoon of liquid glucose is, and whether it should be a heaped or flat tea-spoonful. Don't get worked up! Just remember that if the icing is too dry you can add more liquid, and if it is too wet, then you can add more icing sugar (or, in the case of gelatin icing, more cornflour). It is more important to make icing that will behave as you want it to, rather than to follow instructions slav-ishly. Use your common sense and you won't go wrong.

GELATIN ICING

This is used to make decorative elements that you might want to keep. Although made of entirely edible ingredients, it is assumed that you will not want to eat items made from gelatin icing as it dries like sweet porcelain. It is quick, cheap and easy to make and in certain circumstances can be used instead of petal paste when making flowers (see Poppy Wedding Cake and A Tartan Christmas, pages 75 and 79).

Makes 500g (1lb/2 cups)

15g (½oz/1 sachet) powdered gelatin
10ml (2tsp) liquid glucose
500g (1lb/3 cups) icing sugar
cornflour for dusting

1 Put 60ml (4tbsp) water in a heatproof bowl and sprinkle on the gelatin. Leave to soak for 1 minute, then place the bowl in a saucepan containing 1cm (½ inch) water. Heat gently until the gelatin has dissolved completely. Remove from the heat and stir in the liq-uid glucose. Allow to cool for 1–2 min-utes, and make sure that the glucose has dissolved completely.

2 Put the icing sugar in a bowl, add the gelatin mixture and stir in. If the mix-ture seems very wet, add more icing sugar or some cornflour, a little at a time, until the icing can be worked with your hands like dough. The finished icing should be silky to the touch and not sticky.

3 Wrap the icing immediately in plastic food wrap to stop the icing drying out when in contact with the air. There is no point in storing this icing as it does not mature. Whatever you do, do not store it in the fridge as it will harden like a brick. If left for several hours or longer, unwrap the icing and knead it again on your work surface. The warmth of your hands will soften the gelatin again and the icing will become pliable. If, however, a crust has formed on the icing, do not attempt to knead it into the icing as you will be left with tiny and annoying 'bits' throughout the icing, which will make it unusable. Instead, cut off the crust and continue working with what is left.

4 Gelatin icing is wonderful to use because it is soft and elastic, and will mould beautifully over various shapes (see Cactus Willy and Do It Yourself!, pages 24 and 71, for example). Even better, gelatin icing will not stick to whatever you mould it over, as long as the item is free of grease and is not damp. The icing does not even stick to itself.

MODELLING ICING

For some of the cakes in this book, for example When I Win The Pools (see page 40) and Cadillac (see page 19), we have made figures moulded from 'mod-elling' icing. This is made simply by mixing equal amounts of fondant and gelatin icing together. This gives you the soft, moulding quality of fondant icing combined with the quick-drying facility of gelatin icing. There are other, and rather more complex recipes for modelling icing. If you have a favourite, use that, but this one works perfectly well.

BUTTERCREAM

Buttercream can be made very simply by adding icing sugar to softened butter, adding a little vanilla essence. However, if you want to try something different that is well worth the extra effort, try this French buttercream. You will need to spread this icing on to a cake straight away as it begins to harden as soon as it is made.

Makes 375g (12oz/1½ cups)

4 egg yolks
125g (4oz/⅔ cup) caster sugar
250g (8oz) butter, softened

1 Beat the egg yolks lightly in a bowl until mixed. Put the sugar in a saucepan with 100ml (3½ fl oz) water and heat gently until dissolved. Bring to the boil and boil until the syrup reaches the soft ball stage (115°C/240°F on a sugar thermometer).

2 Gradually pour the hot sugar syrup on to the egg yolks, beating constantly. Continue beating until the mixture is cool and thick.

3 Cream the butter until very soft, and gradually beat it into the egg mixture. Use immediately.

Gelatin icing is easy to handle and can be used to make all sorts of unusual shapes. It dries to a hard, brittle finish and is usually used to make decorations that will be kept rather than eaten.

Cook's tip

Sugar absorbs water; you might even find that humid weather affects the icing you are using. Be careful not to leave iced cakes or icing decorations in a damp atmosphere as the sugar might begin to soften. Do not store cakes in the cold, or if you do be sure not to move them straight into a hot room, as the icing might begin to 'sweat'. For the same reason, don't be tempted to store iced cakes in the fridge.

Cake Boards

Once iced in detail, cakes are very difficult to move around, so it is always best to finish them off on the standard (thick) cake board on which they are to be served. For preliminary covering with marzipan and fondant icing, however, we always recommend using a thin cake board (or card). The cake can then easily be moved from your work surface and left elsewhere to harden, before it is transferred to a standard cake board. To free the cake from the thin board, bend the board gently downwards all around the cake to separate the board from the edges of the fondant. Use a large, rigid-bladed knife to lift the cake carefully from one board to the other.

Covering Cakes

Below, from left: Push the marzipan 'sausage' firmly into the gap between cake and board.

Dust your hands with icing sugar to smooth the marzipan down the sides of the cake.

Applying marzipan and icing to a cake is quite straightforward, unless the cake has a particularly awkward shape. For the cake designs in this book, special instructions are given for covering the more unusually shaped cakes. The following instructions give the basic techniques for covering a single-tier cake with marzipan and icing.

We have used a fruit cake to illustrate these techniques because a surprising number of people are unaware that, when icing a fruit cake for Christmas or a wedding, it is actually the bottom of the cake that is iced. However, there is no need to cut off any cake to make the top even enough to form a stable base. Turn the cake upside down, roll out a sausage-shaped piece of marzipan, and push it into the gap between the cake and the board. Using a flat-bladed knife, trim the marzipan to the edge of the cake, then smooth it to ensure that the sides of the cake are absolutely flat.

Spread the top and sides of the cake with sieved apricot jam. Roll out the marzipan on a work surface lightly dusted with icing sugar and lay the sheet of marzipan over the cake. Using an icing smoother, carefully smooth the marzipan on to the surface of the cake to

make sure it is fixed and that there are no bubbles of air caught underneath. With hands lightly dusted with icing sugar, smooth the marzipan down the sides of the cake. If folds form, simply pull the marzipan away from the sides again and continue smoothing with a light downward pressure until the cake is completely covered. Trim the marzipan to the base of the cake and, using the smoother again, ensure that all surfaces are as neat and flat as possible.

Fondant icing is applied to a cake in exactly the same way as marzipan. Some people suggest brushing the surface of the marzipan with boiled water or alcohol in order to help the icing stick. However, when icing a single-tier cake like this, we never do. Some would argue that brushing with water helps reduce the chance of bubbles being caught under the icing, but we have found the opposite to be true. Fondant icing sticks perfectly well to the marzipan when left for a short time, and the only time we suggest brushing the cake is when gravity dictates that if we didn't the icing would simply fall off, as in Cactus Willy (see page 24).

Below, right: A plastic icing smoother gives a lovely silky finish to fondant icing.

Colouring

The use of strong and vibrant colours is a constant feature throughout this book, so it is worth spending a little time talking about it. A huge variety of food colourings is now available, from the watery, cochineal-type colourings used to produce pale pastel shades in royal icing, to the dense paste colourings that are sold in solid form in little pots. You can also obtain food colouring pens, dusting powders and edible glitters.

Despite the ever-increasing range of colours and shades, very few food colourings produce the shade described on the label when mixed into fondant icing. At a certain point, the colour refuses to deepen, becoming denser instead. In response to this, we often add some colour to the icing to give a uniform base, then apply more colour with a brush after shaping. Food colourings can be blended in just the same way as watercolours. If you can't find the shade you want, try mixing several together. By experimenting, you can often get closer to the exact colour you want than the manufacturer.

Throughout this book, we recommend using paste food colourings. There is a very good reason for this. These concentrated colours allow you to use less colour in order to reach the shade you want, and as a result have less effect on the consistency of the icing. Liquid colourings can make the icing too wet and completely unmanageable by the time you have added enough to give the shade you want.

Until recently, two colours in particular were very difficult to achieve, namely pillar box red and black. New concentrated shades on the market have now made the red entirely possible to achieve, but black is still difficult if you want to mix it in rather than paint it on. You may find that, in the Glass of Stout cake (see Cappuccino Kisses, page 31), for example, you will have to stop at a dark grey and add further depth by painting on lines of black afterwards. Remember, too, that, in the past, black colouring painted on to cakes sometimes remained tacky. This may change according to the brand of colouring you use, but it is just as well to be careful. It is also interesting to note that different materials, i.e. different kinds of icings and marzipan, 'accept' colour in different ways. You need to add less colour to marzipan to achieve the shade you want, than to icing, and marzipan seems to hold a richer colour than icing. On the whole, it is well worth experimenting with different colours and materials before you set out to make a cake.

SPECIAL EFFECTS

In most instances, solid colours are used on the cakes in this book. Every now and again, however, certain simple but special effects have been incorporated in order to brighten things up. Easier than they look, here are a few to try:

WOOD GRAIN Brush the icing with pale brown food colouring and allow it to dry. Coat the bristles of a medium-sized paintbrush in a darker brown, and drag it over the icing to

Using liquid colouring can have very messy results, while paste colourings produce a strong colour and perfectly manageable icing!

Special colouring effects can make all the difference to the finish of a cake, and are not hard to achieve.
Top row, left to right: Wood grain, Stippling, Sponging.
Bottom row, left to right: Marbling, Sponge rolling, Blending.

create a 'grain' effect, swerving to allow for knot holes and using concentric circles to emphasize them.

STIPPLING   Brush your chosen food colouring on to the icing. Reload the brush with the colour and, with the bristles splayed out, dab over the surface to break it up and add texture.

SPONGING   The use of a textured sponge allows for a softer application of colour, which becomes more subtle when the sponge is closer-textured. It is important that the sponge should not be overloaded with colour.

MARBLING   Mix up two or three tones of the same colour (a dark, a medium and a light), and apply each one in turn, blending the edges of the colours together while still wet, so that you end up with a subtly varying series of shades. Leave to dry for 10 minutes. Overpaint fine veins in a darker colour using a very fine paintbrush. Highlight with silver or white, if liked.

SPONGE ROLLING   Using an artist's sponge roller evenly loaded with food colouring, apply gentle pressure while rolling it over the icing to produce textured bands of colour.

BLENDING   Brush together two food colourings that lie side by side while still wet, in order to produce a graduation from one to the other.

Cadillac

Love them or loathe them, cars are a feature of modern living. Life's highspots can sometimes be linked to the memory of a particular car – the one we passed our test in, the first one we ever bought, the one that drove us away to begin married life. Well, in honour of that symbol of freedom, here are two simple but fun ways of having your car and eating it!

YOU WILL NEED

one 25cm (10 inch) square cake (see pages 8–9)
one 30cm (12 inch) thin square cake board
apricot jam, sieved
500g (1lb) marzipan
icing sugar for dusting
1.75kg (3½lb) fondant icing (see page 13)
black, green, yellow, blue, silver, pink, brown
and red paste food colourings
one 38cm (15 inch) standard square cake board
185g (6oz) modelling icing (see page 14)
375g (12oz/1½ cups) gelatin icing (see page 14)
cornflour for dusting

EQUIPMENT
artist's paintbrush
cocktail stick

1 Trace the cadillac outline on page 89 on to greaseproof or non-stick paper. Enlarge it so that it fits snugly within a 25cm (10 inch) square (see page 10). Note that the outline of the car is divided into three sections – A, B and C – by two dotted lines. Be sure to mark these dotted lines on your greaseproof paper as they will be used later on. Cut the outline out around the solid line. Place the cake on a 30cm (12 inch) thin square cake board. Lay the paper template on the cake and cut around it (see photo 1), removing the unwanted cake.

2 Cut the paper template into three pieces along the dotted lines. Place section A of the template in position on the cake, and cut along the top edge, cutting down into the cake to a depth of 1cm (½ inch). Remove the template. Now make a cut along the top of the cake 1cm (½ inch) down the side. Cut in until you meet your first cut. Remove the unwanted piece of cake. Place section B of the template in position and cut along its top edge, cutting down into the cake to a depth of 1cm (½ inch). Remove the template. Again, make another cut along the top of the cake 1cm (½ inch) down the side, cutting in

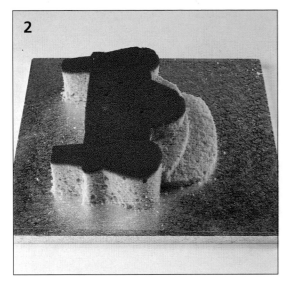

until you meet up with the line you have just cut. Remove the unwanted piece of cake. The top of your car shape has now been carved into three levels (see photo 2). Round down all the angles on the cake to create smoother and more flowing lines.

3 Spread the surface of the cake with apricot jam. Roll out the marzipan on a work surface lightly dusted with icing sugar. Lay the marzipan over the cake, and gently smooth it over the detail, taking extra care around the wheels where you have the greatest depth of cake. Carefully smooth the marzipan down over the wheels and trim away any excess neatly around the edges of the cake. Leave for several hours before proceeding.

4 Trace the design for the cake board on page 88 on to greaseproof or non-stick paper, and enlarge it so that it can be contained neatly within a 38cm (15 inch) square (see page 10). The background detail is created like a jigsaw puzzle – individual pieces of fondant icing are cut out and placed in the appropriate position on the board. Divide 1.1kg (2¼ lb) fondant icing into the following portions and colour as

indicated: 315g (10oz) grey (using black food colouring); 185g (6oz) green; 125g (4oz) yellow; 125g (4oz) dark blue; 185g (6oz) marbled with turquoise (see page 42); 185g (6oz) pale blue. Cut out each piece from your greaseproof paper template in turn and roll out the appropriate shade of fondant icing on a work surface lightly dusted with icing sugar. Cut out the shape and place it in position on the board. Continue until the board is covered (see photo 3). For added effect, silver food colouring can be applied to the top of the mountains and the edges of the waves.

5 To ice the car, colour 440g (14oz) of the remaining fondant icing pink. Roll out the icing on a work surface lightly dusted with icing sugar and lay it over the bonnet and wheels of the car. Gently smooth the icing into position and trim neatly to the edges of the cake. Roll out 125g (4oz) of the remaining white fondant, and lay it over the windscreen. Smooth it into position and trim away any excess. Keep the trimmings and add to the remaining 60g (2oz) white fondant. Roll out this icing and cut out two circles for headlights, and bumper and fender details. Place in position, using a little water to help

Cook's tip

Be careful not to touch the black painted wheels when moving the cake. For some reason, black, when used on large areas, tends to remain tacky. If you are not careful, you might smudge the colour or transfer it on to the background.

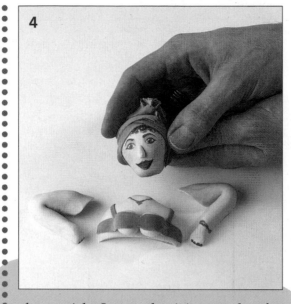

4

them stick. Leave the icing to dry for several hours before proceeding.

6 When the icing is dry, paint the tyres black over the pink fondant, and paint the sides of the wheels with silver food colouring. Paint the bumper and fender details silver, and outline the windscreen and headlights in silver. Those areas that are supposed to be glass, namely the headlights and windscreen, are simply washed over in a thin blue food colouring. Additional fender detail can be added, if you wish, by painting in fine lines of silver to join up the horizontal bars of silver fondant icing, and even more detail by painting in the resulting squares using a deeper shade of pink. Let the colour dry for several hours.

7 One of the figures in the car is moulded, but the second is merely hinted at by simply painting a semi-circle on to the windscreen to indicate the steering wheel, and a few strokes of brown food colouring to suggest a head peering over the wheel. The shadow of the moulded character behind the windscreen is also suggested by the simple addition of a few brushstrokes of pink

to indicate the part of the body that we do not see.

8 Once the colour is dry and the icing firm, remove the cake from the thin board by gently bending the board downwards all round the cake to free it from the icing. Slide a large rigid knife under the cake and lift it carefully into position on the covered cake board.

9 To make the moulded figure, colour the modelling icing a 'flesh' colour or pale pink, and shape it into the required pieces (see photo 4), using 125g (4oz) of the pink icing. Add more pink colour (or another shade altogether) to the remaining 60g (2oz) to make the turban. Simply roll out the icing on a work surface lightly dusted with icing sugar into a piece about 2.5cm (1 inch) wide and 10cm (4 inches) long. Moisten the top of the head with a little water, and wrap the icing piece around the head as decoratively as possible. Leave the icing to firm up for several hours and then paint on the facial details, necklace, bracelet and fingernails. Fix the body together with a little water or royal icing, and place in position on the cake.

10 Trace the outlines for the hotel, palm trees, number plate and 'Just Married' sign on pages 89–90 on to greaseproof or non-stick paper. Enlarge them, if necessary, in proportion to the cadillac shape (see page 10), and cut them out. Roll out the gelatin icing on a work surface lightly dusted with cornflour to a large sheet. Cut out the outlines and use the paper templates to cut out three hotels and three palm trees (plus the two rectangular pieces). For the number plate, and 'Just Married' sign, go over the lettering on the greaseproof paper with the tip of a cocktail stick while the icing is still soft. Let all the pieces of icing dry for several hours.

cocktail stick to represent bricks. This is then covered in 375g (12oz) yellow fondant cut into a 'starburst' shape using the template on page 89. To make the individual bricks, colour some modelling icing terracotta and cut them out using the templates on page 90. Once dry, fix them to the board supported by small pieces of icing or marzipan to lift them up and away from the board. This gives a wonderful feeling of 'flying' bricks!

Perfect for saying 'congratulations on passing your test' to a friend or loved one, the number plate and character on this cake can be varied according to who you are making it for.

11 For the cake illustrated, the hotels are painted in food colours on white icing. (If you prefer, you can colour the icing before rolling it out, and then use a darker shade of the same colour to paint in the windows.) The palm trees are painted in shades of green and brown, with simple brush strokes. The lettering on the number plate and sign are painted over the faint indentations in the icing. Stick the number plate and sign in position using a little water or royal icing. The hotels and palm trees are fixed to the board with a small piece of marzipan or icing underneath the bottom end so that each piece in turn tilts upwards, creating a feeling of distance (see photo 5).

VARIATION

The 'L Driver' cake is made and decorated in exactly the same way but the cake board is covered in 750g (1½ lb) terracotta-coloured fondant icing (achieved by mixing dark brown, Christmas red and egg yellow), which is then simply scored while soft using a

Cactus Willy

Is it love or just infatuation? Sometimes it is difficult to tell the difference. Either way, you simply can't stop thinking about that special person. Anything and everything you see reminds you of them, or part of them, and even a humble cactus can be filled with erotic potential. Cactus Willy is a naughty, tongue-in-cheek way to send your own special message to a loved one.

The following instructions give quantities for making either Cactus Willy or Bosoms. If you wish to make both, simply double the quantities.

YOU WILL NEED
two 15cm (6 inch) round cakes (see pages 8–9)
1.1kg (2¼lb) marzipan
icing sugar for dusting
apricot jam, sieved
500g (1lb) fondant icing (see page 13)
dark brown, Christmas red, egg yellow, dark green and silver paste food colourings
one 25cm (10 inch) standard round cake board
250g (8oz/1 cup) gelatin icing (see page 14)
cornflour for dusting
dark soft brown sugar
royal icing (optional)

EQUIPMENT
ruler
string for measuring
icing smoother
artist's paintbrush
cocktail sticks
a small, clean garden fork
red ribbon

1 Spread the filling of your choice on one cake and place the second cake on top (see page 11). Using a large, sharp, rigid-bladed knife, gently shave

off pieces of cake, shaping the sides so they slope gently and evenly in towards the base (see photo 1). Leave the top of the cake intact.

2 Roll out 625g (1¼lb) marzipan on a surface lightly dusted with icing sugar. Spread the sides and top of the cake with apricot jam. Using the base of the tin the cakes were baked in as a guide, cut out a circle of marzipan and place it on top of the cake. Measure the depth of the cake with a ruler and use a

An even cheekier message for the gift tag could be 'A Prize Specimen!' or 'You Can Grow Anything'

piece of string to measure the circumference of the top of the cake. Cut out a rectangle of marzipan that matches these measurements and press it against the sides of the cake (an extra pair of hands is useful at this point). Continue pressing on the marzipan all the way round the cake, cutting away any excess and leaving one neat seam. Smooth the marzipan firmly into position with a plastic icing smoother. (If you can't get any help and find one piece of marzipan too difficult to manage, cut the rectangle into two pieces. This will make it easier to handle, but will give you two seams. Allow the marzipan to dry for several hours.

3 Colour the fondant icing a shade of terracotta. To achieve this colour, mix some dark brown paste colouring with Christmas red (or similar) and egg yellow. Brush the marzipan on the sides of the cake with boiled water and roll out the terracotta icing on a work surface dusted with icing sugar. Measure the cake again and cut the icing into a rectangle that is as wide as the depth of the cake, and long enough to wrap around it (see photo 2). Re-roll the icing trimmings and cut a second rectangle of icing, this time long enough to wrap around the top of the cake and about 3.5cm (1½ inches) wide. Gently lift the

large rectangle of icing and press it around the cake. (Again, an extra pair of hands is helpful here.) Using a smoother, carefully press the icing into position. (As with the marzipan, the icing can be applied in two pieces if you find it easier, which will leave you with two seams.) Trim the icing neatly so that the ends join together as cleanly as possible. Moisten the top 2.5cm (1 inch) of the cake with boiled water. (Be sparing: if you use too wet a paintbrush or pastry brush you might find that water dribbles down the sides of the cake.) Wrap the second icing strip around the top of the 'pot' so that it stands about 1cm (½ inch) above the top of the cake. This gives a more realistic finish to the cake, but you have to be as neat as possible when fixing it into position. (Once again, this can be done in two pieces, but make sure the seams marry up with the seams on the pot sides.) Place the cake on the cake board with the icing seam at the back. (If your cake has two seams, position it so the seams are at the sides.)

4 To make the willy, colour the remaining 500g (1lb) marzipan 'cactus' green. To achieve this colour, mix some dark green paste food colouring with a little dark brown. Divide the marzipan into three pieces, one weighing 315g (10oz) and two weighing 90g (3oz) each. Roll the larger piece on a work surface lightly dusted with icing sugar until it resembles a cucumber measuring about 15cm (6 inches) long. Shape the ends so that one is rounded and the other flat. Using the end of a paintbrush (or something similar), score lines at intervals down the length of the marzipan. Stand it up on its flat end and leave it to dry for several hours. Roll the two remaining pieces of marzipan into balls, flatten them slightly, and score with lines. Leave to dry.

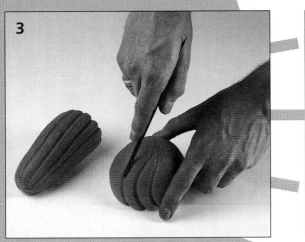

5 To make bosoms, reserve two tiny pieces of marzipan and colour the remainder 'cactus' green in the same way. Divide the green marzipan into two equal pieces. Roll the pieces into slightly peaked mounds and score in curving lines with the end of a paintbrush (see photo 3). Colour the two tiny pieces of marzipan bright red, shape into 'pips' and fix one on top of each bosom. Use the end of a paintbrush to mark dots in the green marzipan around the red 'pips'. (For an authentic cactus finish, you can cut off the ends of cocktail sticks, paint them with green food colouring, and when dry, push them into the bosoms in groups of three, but this is not strictly necessary.) Allow the marzipan to dry for several hours before putting into position.

6 To make the garden fork, roll out a thin sheet of gelatin icing on a work surface lightly dusted with cornflour. Place the icing over a real fork and gently mould it into the detail of the fork (see photo 4). Using a sharp knife, trim away the excess icing, reserving the trimmings to make the gift tag if required. Leave for 6–8 hours to allow the icing to harden, then carefully remove the icing from the fork and paint it with red and silver food colourings. Leave to dry.

7 To assemble the cake, place the willy pieces on top of the 'pot' and spoon brown sugar around them to represent soil. Place the fork in position on the board by the side of the 'pot', fixing it with a little royal icing if required.

8 Cut out a gift tag, either from card or from a rolled-out piece of gelatin icing. If you are using icing and want to eat the label, trace the message of your choice (see page 91) on to greaseproof or non-stick paper, and enlarge it as necessary (see page 10). Lay it over the icing tag and score over the message with the end of a cocktail stick while the icing is still soft enough to take an imprint. Make a hole in the tag for the ribbon. When the icing is dry, paint the message with red food colouring. If you are using a card label, or if you do not intend eating the label, trace the message on to greaseproof or non-stick paper, then transfer it to the label by going over it again with a piece of carbon or graphite paper between the traced message and the label.

9 Thread a piece of red ribbon through the gift tag and carefully loop it around Cactus Willy.

> ## Cook's tip
> Be careful not to overhandle marzipan. The warmth of your hands will bring the almond oil to the surface, making the marzipan sticky. Also, if the marzipan is too warm after shaping, it can settle slightly before it firms up, which means it could lose some of its shape.

21-Bum Salute

There are times in life when an anniversary or celebration should be made public and the message trumpeted loud and clear. The Queen has the right idea – she lets off a thundering fusillade across Hyde Park, making everyone stop and take notice. Given that we cannot all have a troop of cavalry disporting themselves in the back garden, here is a cheeky play on words where 'Gun Salute' becomes 'Bum Salute', and every celebration is immortalized in a bold bevy of bumptious bottoms!

YOU WILL NEED

one 25cm (10 inch) round cake (see pages 8–9)
one 38cm (15 inch) standard round cake board
apricot jam, sieved
1.25kg (2½lb) marzipan
icing sugar for dusting
1.25kg (2½lb) fondant icing (see page 13)
one 18cm (7 inch) round cake (see pages 8–9)
one 25cm (10 inch) thin round cake board
3kg (6lb) modelling icing (see page 14)
assorted paste food colourings
royal icing (see page 13)
red powder food colouring

EQUIPMENT
cocktail sticks
artist's paintbrush
flower cutters
plastic drinking straws

1 Place the large cake on the cake board, brush it with apricot jam, and cover it with marzipan and fondant icing (see page 16). You will need 750g (1½ lb) marzipan and 750g (1½ lb) fondant icing. Place the smaller cake on the thin cake board and cover it with 500g (1lb) marzipan and 500g (1lb) fondant icing. Allow both cakes to rest for 6–8 hours or overnight to give the icing time to harden.

2 To remove the smaller cake from the thin board, simply lift the cake and board up off the work surface and gently ease the board downwards, working gradually all around the cake. This should separate the icing from the board and allow you to slide a large rigid knife under the cake, and move it into position on top of the larger cake. (Leaving the icing to harden is important as it makes moving the cakes easier, and ensures that you don't leave fingerprints or other marks in the icing.)

3 Each of the 21 bottoms on this cake is made using about 125g (4oz) modelling icing. This leaves about 375g (12oz) modelling icing to make the knickers, boxer shorts, etc. (Obviously, you may choose to increase or decrease these amounts if you wish to do more or less elaborate clothing or figures. It is also possible to mould the bottoms out of marzipan. This would allow you to keep them, if you wish, or to enjoy eating them, but has obvious consequences in terms of cost.)

Cook's tip
This two-tier cake is arranged in the American style, that is with a smaller cake placed straight on top of a larger one. It could be made with just one cake, but the additional tier gives extra height and makes it easier to arrange the bottoms in amusing positions.

4 To make the bottoms, colour each piece of modelling icing individually, varying the colours for added humour. Shape each piece into a pear shape, and then, using the end of a paintbrush or something similar, score a line around the fat end of each piece of icing to produce the cheeks of the bottom (see photo 1). Arrange the bottoms on and around the cake one at a time, dressing each one before positioning the next. If you try to dress the bottoms after you have put them all on the cake, you might find it difficult to get into all the corners. Use a little royal icing to fix the bottoms securely in position on and around the cake.

5 To dress the bottoms, colour the remaining modelling icing in various bright and contrasting colours. Photo 2 shows simple shapes and design ideas for swimming costumes, boxer shorts, Y fronts and frilled leotards. Dressing the bottoms is your opportunity to personalize the cake. If the recipient of the cake favours one particular kind of underwear (much to your disapproval, or perhaps to your delight!) or perhaps has fantasies about the kind he or she would like you to wear, here is your opportunity to make a statement.

6 Use red powder food colouring to dust a lovely blush on to some of the bottoms. For details on how to make a frill, see the Medallion Man cake on page 65. The flower shapes are made by using a simple plunger cutter, and dots by using a plastic drinking straw. Press the end of the straw into some rolled-out icing. If the icing piece gets stuck in the end of the straw, gently blow it out on to the work surface. Brush the backs of dots and flowers with a tiny amount of water, and press gently on to items of clothing, then position the clothing on the bottoms, securing with a little more water. Fill any gaps between the bottoms on the cake with pieces of modelling icing, coloured, rolled out and shaped to resemble draped towels.

Cappuccino Kisses

Holding hands at a pavement café while staring intently into each other's eyes – is it your imagination or is even your cup of coffee falling under the spell? Love is all around and hearts abound. Here is a whimsical way to express your love in a wonderfully simple creation that makes words unnecessary.

YOU WILL NEED

two 20cm (8 inch) round cakes (see pages 8–9)
apricot jam, sieved
one 30cm (12 inch) thin round cake board
1kg (2lb) marzipan
icing sugar for dusting
1.25kg (2½lb) fondant icing (see page 13)
one 30cm (12 inch) standard round cake board
1 large egg white
60g (2oz/½ cup) caster sugar
500g (1lb/2 cups) gelatin icing (see page 14)
cornflour for dusting
blue, red, pink, silver and brown paste food colourings
royal icing (see page 13)
demerara sugar (optional)

EQUIPMENT

string for measuring
cocktail stick
non-stick baking paper
dinner plate
large serving spoon
2.5cm (1 inch) artist's sponge roller or household paintbrush
artist's paintbrush
thin card

1 Sandwich the two cakes together with apricot jam. Using a large, sharp, rigid-bladed knife, cut the top edge of the cake off, holding the knife at an angle of 45° to the surface of the cake (see photo 1).

2 Place the cake on a 30cm (12 inch) thin round cake board, and spread the top and the cut edge of the cake with apricot jam. Roll out 250g (8oz) marzipan on a work surface dusted with icing sugar, and drape it over the top of the cake. Smooth the marzipan into position, then trim off the excess neatly, level with the bottom of the sloping edge. Reserve the trimmings.

3 Use a piece of string to measure the depth and circumference of the cake. Spread the sides of the cake with apricot jam. Roll out 500g (1lb) of the remaining marzipan, together with the trimmings, into a rectangle that is as wide as the depth of the cake, and long enough to fit around it (see photo 2). Fix this to the sides of the cake and smooth into position. (If you feel the rectangle of marzi-

31

pan is too large to handle in one go, cut it into two pieces and position them one at a time, but be sure that the resulting seams are as neat as possible.) Allow the cake to rest for several hours to give the marzipan time to firm up.

4 Turn the cake upside down and spread the base with apricot jam. Roll out the remaining marzipan together with any trimmings. Using the tin in which the cakes were baked as a guide, cut out a circle that will fit neatly on the base of the cake. Smooth gently into position and leave for several hours before turning the cake over.

5 The cake is covered with fondant icing in almost exactly the same way as it is covered with marzipan. Moisten the marzipan on the top of the cake and on the sloping edges by brushing with a little boiled water. Roll out 250g (8oz) fondant icing on a work surface lightly dusted with icing sugar. Drape the icing over the moistened marzipan and smooth it into position. Trim the icing to the bottom of the sloping edge, reserving the trimmings. Allow to dry for several hours. (This iced surface of the cake will in fact be the bottom of the cup when it is positioned on the saucer.)

6 Measure the depth and circumference of the cake with a piece of string. Roll out 500g (1lb) of the remain-

ing fondant icing, together with the trimmings, and cut out a rectangle that is long enough to fit around the cake, and 1cm (½ inch) wider than the depth of the cake. Brush the marzipan on the sides of the cake with a little boiled water. Rather than trying to lift the rectangle of icing into position on the sides of the cake, it is easier to lift the cake and to roll it along the icing, pressing the icing into position as you go. Line up the cake so that the bottom edge of the sloped top is in line with one long edge of the icing (see photo 3). Return the iced cake to the cake board.

7 While the icing is still soft, trace the 'Café d'Amour' design on page 91 on to greaseproof or non-stick paper, enlarge it in proportion to the cup (see page 10), and transfer it to the icing on the side of the cup. To do this, hold the design against the icing and go over the outline with the end of a cocktail stick, leaving an impression in the soft icing. Leave the icing to harden.

8 Roll out the remaining 500g (1lb) fondant icing and use it to cover the 30cm (12 inch) standard round cake board, trimming off excess.

9 To make the frothy 'cappuccino' topping for the cake, whisk the egg white in a bowl until stiff. Add half the caster sugar, 1 teaspoon at a time,

whisking between each addition to make sure the meringue stays stiff and glossy. Finally, fold in the remaining caster sugar using a large metal spoon. Lay a piece of non-stick baking paper over the top of the cake. Using a pencil or food colouring pen, draw a circle on the paper the same size as the top of the cake. Remove the paper from the cake, turn it over and lay it on a flat surface. Spread the meringue on the paper, keeping within the circle and making a slight mound in the centre (see photo 4). Place the paper on a baking sheet and bake in the oven at 120°C (250°F/Gas ½) for 1–1½ hours or until the meringue is a pale beige colour. Take out of the oven and allow to cool.

10 Roll out 250g (8oz/1 cup) gelatin icing on a surface lightly dusted with cornflour. Lift the icing on to a dinner plate and smooth it into the shape of the plate. Using a sharp knife, trim away the excess icing from around the plate. Reserve the trimmings. While the icing is still soft, transfer the 'Café d'Amour' symbol on to the edge of the plate in the same way as for the cup (see step 7 on page 32).

11 Roll out 185g (6oz/¾ cup) of the remaining gelatin icing to a thin sheet. Cover a large serving spoon with the icing and smooth it into the shape of

the spoon. Trim the icing neatly to the edge of the spoon, reserving the trimmings. Knead together the remaining 60g (2oz/¼ cup) gelatin icing and the trimmings, and roll into a small piece approximately 1cm (½ inch) thick. Cut and shape this into a handle for the cup. Allow all the pieces to dry overnight.

12 To colour the icing on the cake board, dilute some blue paste food colouring with a little water on a plate. Roll a 2.5cm (1 inch) artist's sponge roller in the colour until the roller is coated, and then gently but firmly roll the roller back and forth over the icing to produce a checked design (see photo 5). (If you do not have, or cannot find, a sponge roller, an ordinary household paintbrush would work just as well. If you prefer, you can colour the fondant icing before covering the board.)

13 Using red paste food colouring diluted with water, paint the 'Café d'Amour' designs on the cup and saucer. Paint a stripe in a contrasting colour around the saucer and the top of the cup. Outline the coloured areas with a thin line of silver, and paint a silver line down the centre of the handle. Remove the hardened gelatin icing from the spoon, and paint it silver. Leave to dry.

14 To assemble the cake, lift the gelatin icing 'saucer' off the dinner plate and place it on the iced cake board. Remove the cake from the thin board, gently bending the board downwards all around the base of the cake, if necessary, to free the cake from the board. Place the cake gently on the saucer. Fix the handle in position using dabs of royal icing, then place the meringue circle on top of the cup.

15 Finally, cut a heart shape out of the centre of a piece of thin card, using the outline (enlarged) on page 90. Place the card on top of the meringue and, using an artist's paintbrush and some brown food colouring, gently stipple all over the meringue in the centre. Do not aim for a complete brown covering as this would be too heavy. Instead, make the stippling somewhat uneven, even lightly broken up, for a more authentic appearance. Place the spoon in the saucer and add a little demerara sugar, if liked.

VARIATION

Mine's A Pint or
*The Quickest Way To A
Man's Heart*

Like the cakes for Cactus Willy and 'Do It Yourself!' (see pages 24 and 71), this pint of stout cake is carved very simply. The fondant icing is coloured with black food colouring. With so large a piece of icing, it is almost impossible to achieve a uniform black without making the icing sticky and unmanageable; the best you can achieve is a dark grey. This is fine, as you can later add highlights of black by simply painting vertical bands of black down the sides of the glass to represent light hitting the sides. Thin lines of silver by the side of the black also emphasize the effect of light.

The meringue topping for the stout is made in exactly the same way as for Cappuccino Kisses, except that it needs to be thicker. The head of the stout is also wonderfully white, so set your oven at its lowest setting to dry out the meringue without colouring it, and be prepared to leave it for 2–3 hours, perhaps longer. Before removing it from the oven, take the meringue off its backing of non-stick baking paper. If it is at all soft or weeps sugar syrup, leave it upside down and return it to the oven to dry out.

Transfer the 'Bittersweet' emblem on page 90 to the side of the glass in the same way as the 'Café d'Amour' design is put on the cup for Cappuccino Kisses. Make the beer mat from gelatin icing, using the design on page 91, and following the instructions for making Cactus Willy's gift tag (see page 27).

Cook's tip

For real authenticity, shape the meringue topping so it slopes outwards at the top, as the froth on a glass of stout would.

Is your loved one as dark and mysterious as the glass of stout he enjoys so much? Get his attention with this amusing cake – an affectionate dig suitable for any occasion.

Naughty Cupid

According to the Old Masters and modern-day advertising moguls, behind every wispy cloud is an impish child with wings, a fat tummy and a bare bottom, who is intent on changing your life with a playfully aimed dart. When you least expect it, he will loose one of his arrows and suddenly everything will be hearts and flowers, roses and champagne. Only the hardened cynic would dodge one of Cupid's arrows, so go on, let the chubby imp do his mischief. After all, you never know where it might lead.

YOU WILL NEED

one 30cm (12 inch) square cake (see pages 8–9)
one 30cm (12 inch) thin round cake board
1.25kg (2½lb) fondant icing (see page 13)
icing sugar for dusting
one 38cm (15 inch) standard round cake board
apricot jam, sieved
500g (1lb) marzipan
pink or 'flesh', red, blue and egg yellow paste
food colourings
pink and blue dusting powders
250g (8oz/1 cup) gelatin icing (see page 14)
cornflour for dusting
royal icing (see page 13)

EQUIPMENT
artist's paintbrush
short length of thread

1 Trace the 'Cupid' design on page 92 on to a sheet of greaseproof or non-stick paper, following the outline of the body and head only. Enlarge it so that it will fit snugly within the 30cm (12 inch) square cake (see page 10). Note that three of Cupid's four limbs are well extended so the figure is carved out of the cake on the diagonal. Place the cake on a 30cm (12 inch) thin round cake board. Cut out the enlarged Cupid design and lay it over the cake. Cut away the cake from around the paper (see photo 1).

2 In order to give the cake a sense of movement, the extended arm and leg of the Cupid are carved so that they appear to be pointing into the distance. To achieve this effect with the leg, start carving the sponge away just above the knee. Working towards the foot, cut the sponge in a gradual slope, leaving only a thin piece of cake for the foot. For the arm, start at the shoulder and carve gently down towards the hand.

Additional movement can be created by twisting the trunk slightly. To do this, gently carve a sloping edge along the side between the extended arm and leg. This gives the appearance of the body twisting away from the viewer's eye. The head is also looking slightly away. From a line down the centre of the head, carve out and gently down to the left (see photo 2). The only other detail that requires carving is the second leg, which is bent back. For the top of the leg, from thigh to knee, leave the complete depth of the cake. For the calf behind, carve away half the thickness of the cake. Finally, for the foot, carve away three-quarters of the thickness of the cake. In order to give the figure a more rounded, elegant appearance, round off the remaining angles with a knife and gently undercut the base of the cake.

3 Roll out 750g (1½lb) fondant icing on a surface lightly dusted with icing sugar, and lay it over the 38cm (15 inch) round cake board. Trim any excess icing neatly away from the edge of the board, and gently smooth the icing into as flat and perfect a surface as possible. Leave for several hours before proceeding with the clouds.

4 Carefully spread the cake with apricot jam. Roll out the marzipan on a work surface lightly dusted with icing sugar and lay it over the cake. Smooth the marzipan down over the cake, paying particular attention to the space between the front extended arm and leg. This part of the cake is quite narrow and deep, and you may find that your marzipan will not stretch without breaking. If this happens, do not worry: simply patch up any uncovered areas of cake with pieces of marzipan left over after trimming. Leave for about 2 hours before proceeding.

5 Colour the remaining fondant icing either a soft pink or flesh colour and roll it out on a surface lightly dusted with icing sugar. Lay the icing over the cake and smooth it gently into the features, once again paying particular attention to the narrow space between the front extended arm and leg. If the icing cracks or splits, simply patch any uncovered parts with small pieces of extra icing. If you look at the photo of the finished cake (page 37), you will see that any patching in this area can be disguised or even covered up with a flowing robe. Trim the icing neatly around the base of the cake.

6 To paint the clouds on the board, follow the instructions given for My Heart Has Wings on page 60. For a slightly different effect, you can use a different cloud shape (see the outline on pages 92–93). Once the colours have dried on the clouds, remove the cake from the board it is on and place it gently in position on the cloud-covered board. To do this, carefully bend the thin board downwards to free it from the icing all around the cake. Slide a large, rigid-bladed knife under the Cupid and place it carefully on the cloud background.

Cook's tip

As with all cakes that require carving, if you prefer detail can be added by building up with marzipan in combination with some carving, rather than trying to carve in every detail.

7 The details of the face are painted very simply in a series of brief, pale brown lines to outline the bow-like lips, the eyebrows, eyes and nose. Other features, such as the navel, toes and fingers, can simply be painted on in the same way. The cheeks and subtle shading on other parts of the body are achieved by dusting the relevant areas with food colouring powders. Use powder to emphasize shadows on the limbs, under the chest and around the tummy, and down the sides of the underarms and thighs.

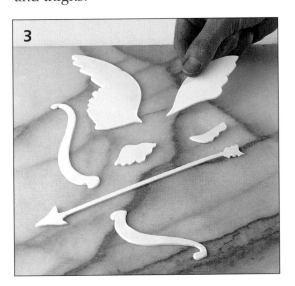

8 Roll out 125g (4oz/½ cup) gelatin icing on a surface lightly dusted with cornflour. Trace the illustrations of the bow, arrow and wing shapes on page 92 on to a piece of greaseproof or non-stick paper, enlarge them in proportion to the Cupid (see page 10), cut them out and use them to cut out the shapes from the icing. Cut the bow into two halves, then leave all the pieces to harden for several hours (see photo 3). Paint the bow and arrow, and the wings, in colours of your choice.

9 Colour the remaining gelatin icing pink. Roll it out into an oblong and gather it into loose folds. Arrange it

gently over the Cupid, sticking it into position with a little water.

10 Fix the bow, arrow and wings in position with a little water. Tie a short length of thread around the ends of the bow, and loop it around the flight of the arrow.

11 For the hair, make up a small amount of royal icing using just half an egg white (see page 13). The icing should not be too thick as it needs to be applied with an artist's paintbrush, but it needs to be stiff enough to hold its shape. Paint some on a saucer or plate before putting it on the cake to see if it will hold its shape sufficiently. Colour the icing a wonderful golden colour using egg yellow food colouring, and then simply 'paint' it over the head in a series of swirls to give the impression of curls (see photo 4). Leave to dry for about 30 minutes.

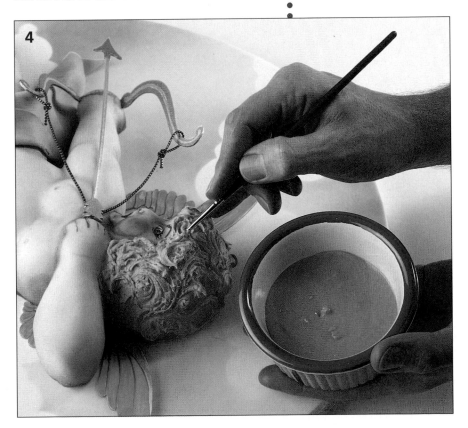

When I Win the Pools

It only happens in television soap operas, or does it? Just lay back and imagine warm perfumed water sensuously bathing your fabulous body, as a god-like creature ministers to your every need, gently massaging you with fragrant oils, feeding you with peeled grapes and pouring you chilled champagne. Ah yes! Yes? No! Oh well, it's a nice dream, and this cake can help you make it come true, or alternatively you can have a giggle with our closer-to-the-truth version. The instructions given below are for making the 'fantasy' version of this cake. The 'reality' version is made in a very similar way, though there are some major differences (see page 45).

YOU WILL NEED

one 25cm (10 inch) square cake (see pages 8–9)
one 38cm (15 inch) standard square cake board
apricot jam, sieved
1kg (2lb) marzipan
icing sugar for dusting
1kg (2lb) fondant icing (see page 13)
rose pink, brown, yellow and blue paste food colourings
500g (1lb) modelling icing (see page 14)
royal icing, see page 13 (optional)
155g (5oz/1 cup) icing sugar
250g (8oz/1 cup) gelatin icing (see page 14)

EQUIPMENT
ruler
wedding cake pillars (optional)
gauzy fabric (optional)
plastic ornaments (optional)

1 Place the cake on the cake board, positioning it slightly towards the back. Make a vertical cut in the top of the cake parallel with one of the two adjacent front edges, 2.5cm (1 inch) in from the edge and to a depth of 1cm (½ inch). Next, make a horizontal cut in the same side of the cake, 1cm (½ inch) down from the top, cutting into the side until you meet the first cut. Remove the resulting unwanted piece of cake. Repeat on the second side. You have now carved one step.

Next, make a vertical cut 1cm (½ inch) in from the edge of the first step on one side to a depth of 1cm (½ inch). Make another horizontal cut 1cm (½ inch) down the side of the cake and in to a depth of 1cm (½ inch) or until you meet the first cut. Remove the piece of cake and repeat on the second side. You will now have carved a second step in two sides of the cake (see photo 1).

Cook's tip
This cake is improved if the cake is turned upside down on the board and the smooth bottom surface used as the top. To even up the sides, fill the gap between cake and board with a 'sausage' of marzipan (see page 16).

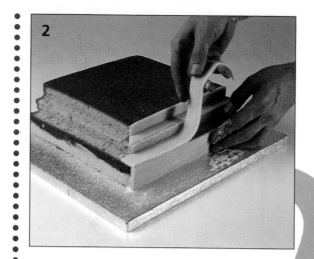

2 To begin covering the cake with marzipan, start with the steps. Spread the steps with apricot jam. Roll out the marzipan on a work surface lightly dusted with icing sugar, and begin by cutting strips of marzipan to the length and depth of each step, using a ruler and a sharp knife. Lay the strips in position one at a time, keeping the seams as neat as possible to keep the edges sharp (see photo 2).

3 To carve the bath, begin by using the tip of a knife to score an oval shape in the top of the cake. To make the scene more interesting, arrange the oval on the diagonal. Make sure that you leave at least 1cm (½ inch) of cake all around the bath. Cut down to a depth of 2.5cm (1 inch), following your scored line as a guide, then cut out the oval shape to a depth of 2.5cm (1 inch).

4 To cover the top of the cake, cut out a piece of marzipan that is about 1cm (½ inch) larger all round than the top of the cake. This will allow for the additional marzipan needed to cover the inside of the bath. Spread the whole of the top of the cake with apricot jam and place the marzipan over it. Smooth it gently into position, ensuring that the inside of the bath is covered. Trim the

edges neatly. Finally, spread the other two straight sides of the cake with apricot jam and cut out two pieces of marzipan big enough to cover them. Attach to the sides of the cake, trimming as neatly as possible, particularly along the edges of the steps. Allow the marzipan to firm up for several hours before proceeding.

5 The cake is iced with fondant icing coloured to resemble marble, except for the inside of the bath which is plain white. Set aside 185g (6oz) white fondant icing for the bath. The simplest way to achieve a marble effect when colouring fondant icing is to add 2–3 sizeable dabs of paste food colouring (rose pink in this case) and to fold the icing over the colour, kneading it on a surface lightly dusted with icing sugar. The idea is to knead the colour in only lightly so that swirls of colour are left in the icing. If in doubt, stop kneading sooner rather than later, otherwise you might end up with icing that is a uniform colour all over.

6 Follow the same method for covering the steps and sides of the cake with icing as for covering with marzipan (see photo 3), except that the icing should be stuck in position with a little boiled water brushed on to the marzipan. Once again, try to make seams as neat as possible to emphasize the sharp edges of the steps.

Cook's tip

After rolling out marbled fondant icing, take a look at the underside of the rolled out sheet. Interestingly, although the icing might seem rather thin, very often the pattern is totally different on both sides; one side might seem a little dull and uninspiring, while the other could be covered in colourful details and swirls. You can then choose which side you prefer to work with.

7 Before covering the top of the cake, roll out the reserved white icing and use it to line the inside of the bath, trimming the excess away neatly. Roll out the remaining marbled pink icing and drape it over the top of the cake. Cut out the oval shape of the bath, then smooth the pink icing into position, trimming it neatly to meet the edges of the icing lining the bath and at the edge of the top step.

8 To make the figures, divide the modelling icing into two portions, one of 315–375g (10–12oz), for the male, and the other of 125–185g (4–6oz), for the partially submerged female. Colour the two pieces separately. In the cake illustrated, the female is coloured using rose pink to give her a delicate hue, while the male is more bronzed. Add a little brown, and even a touch of yellow, to the rose pink to achieve a more sunkissed tone.

9 Separate the larger piece of icing into pieces required to make the male figure (see photo 4). This might seem somewhat complicated, but is a great deal easier than it looks. Each leg is created simply by rolling out a fingerlength piece of icing, applying slightly more pressure at one end so that the resulting piece is fatter at one end than the other. Using your thumb and forefinger, make a pinch halfway down each leg to make kneecaps. Make another pinch towards the bottom of the narrow end of each leg to make ankles. These simple moves will narrow the legs at the appropriate places to produce the calves, and to throw out the shapes of the thighs. Note that one leg is fully extended and the other bent at the knee. The arms are rolled in the same way, but are of course shorter. Pinch in elbows and wrists to give definition. Once again, one arm is fully extended,

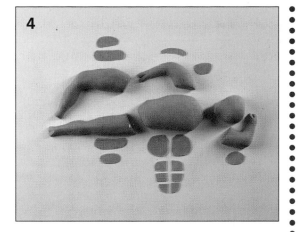

and the other bent at the elbow so that it will eventually support the head. Shape the torso as shown in the photo, allowing for a broad chest and a narrow waist and hips. The head is a simple ball of icing with a snout pinched in, and the ears are two flat triangles of icing. The muscles are cut out of thinly rolled-out icing, and then simply stuck in position using a little water. The only remaining details are a simple bow tie at the neck, and the remaining male equipment. This pig is a real poseur and proud of everything he has!

When all the pieces have been made to your satisfaction, fix them in position using a little water or royal icing. To ensure that all the pieces stick together, apply gentle pressure when fixing in position.

The female figure consists of a head, half torso with bosoms, two arms and one partial bent leg. These pieces can be made and shaped in the same way as for the male.

10 To assemble the cake, fix the female figure in position in the bath and the male figure by the side of the bath, using water or a little royal icing. Make up some glacé icing by mixing the 155g (5oz/1 cup) icing sugar to a runny consistency with a little water. Colour it blue and spoon it around the female figure in the bath.

5

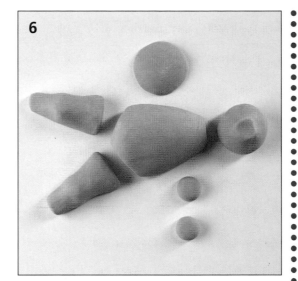

6

11 The remaining details, such as the towels, bowl of fruit, bottle of champagne and the jug pouring the water, are all made from gelatin icing. The icing is simply cut out or moulded and painted with food colour. Although not strictly necessary, these details do add to the overall feeling of luxury, and are also an excellent way of personalizing the cake. If, for example, the person for whom you are making the cake likes a particular fruit, this could be strewn all around the bath. If he or she reads a particular magazine, or has a particular toy for the bath, these details could also be added. For the bottles of bath oils and perfumes, use the shapes on pages 40–45 as a guide.

12 Wedding cake pillars, a plastic pot plant, miniature plastic statues, and a piece of gauzy material can all be added to the surround to create a setting and atmosphere. None of these things is essential, but all add to the sense of fun. Other optional finishing touches include a line of silver around the rim of the bath, and a fancy trailing turban on the female figure's head (made from trimmings of gelatin or fondant icing).

VARIATION

Reality!

The closer-to-the truth version of this cake is made in a very similar way. One major difference, however, is in the shape the original cake must be cut into, and in the shape of the bath (see photo 5). For this design, you might need slightly more gelatin icing in order to allow you to roll out two sheets which can be used to make the back walls. The tiles around the bath are simply made by covering the sides of the bath in one sheet of fondant icing, and then scoring lines horizontally and vertically in the icing with a cocktail stick. It is advisable to allow the icing to harden for several hours before scoring in order to ensure that you end up with sharp lines. The male character has his modesty covered by an all-consuming white vest. However, if you mould one larger and two smaller mounds of modelling icing to represent the stomach and somewhat saggy pectorals, you end up with a more humorous character (see photo 6). Secure the extra pieces to the figure before adding the vest.

Cook's tip

When using glacé icing, do remember that if any bubbles appear on the surface of the icing immediately after spooning it on, prick them out straight away using a needle or pin. Whatever you do, do not be tempted to try to burst them with your finger. Although the surface of the icing seems to harden, it in fact only develops a thin crust, while the icing underneath stays soft and runny. Using your finger will just crack the crust and create a nasty hole.

Opposite: The 'reality' version of this cake will bring you down to earth with a bump – or a splash! Let your imagination run wild and give everyone a good laugh!

The One That Got Away

Sitting on a riverbank for hours on end with nothing to show for it is one of the strangest of popular sporting pastimes. Or at least that's how fishing might seem to those who do not share the passion. Nevertheless, even if no catch is landed, the size of 'the one that got away' is legendary. The theme of this cake allows the pursued to take revenge on the pursuer – sweet revenge indeed! Drop a heavy hint to your loved one by changing the message to suit the occasion. This is one fishy tale that will stand the retelling!

YOU WILL NEED

one 25cm (10 inch) round cake (see pages 8–9)
one 36cm (14 inch) standard round cake board
apricot jam, sieved
2kg (4lb) marzipan
icing sugar for dusting
750g (1½lb) fondant icing (see page 13)
blue, pink, black, green and brown paste food colourings
food colouring and lustre powders
1 egg white, lightly beaten (optional)
250g (8oz/1 cup) gelatin icing, see page 14 (optional)
cornflour for dusting
royal icing (see page 13)

EQUIPMENT

artist's paintbrush
teaspoon
wooden kebab skewers (satay sticks)
florist's tape
florist's wire
cocktail stick

1 Place the cake on the cake board and spread all over with apricot jam. Roll out 1kg (2lb) marzipan on a surface lightly dusted with icing sugar and use to cover the cake (see page 16), trimming away the excess from around the base. Reserve the trimmings.

2 Colour the fondant icing blue and roll it out on a surface lightly dusted with icing sugar. Brush the marzipan on the cake all over with boiled water and drape the icing over it. Smooth carefully into place, trimming away the extra icing from around the base.

3 All the decoration for this cake is made from marzipan. This may seem extravagant; obviously fondant or modelling icing could be used instead, but it is worth experimenting with other materials occasionally, just to see what different effects can be created.

4 The fish is made in two separate pieces to heighten the impression of a cheeky creature taunting the miserable fisherman. Mould 375g (12oz) marzipan into the shape of a fish head. Mark a smile on the fish's head with the end of a paintbrush or the tip of a spoon. Fashion the tail from another 375g (12oz) marzipan, making large tail fins which twist in opposite directions to give the impression of movement.

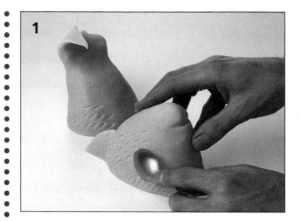

5 Use a little more marzipan to make fins for the back and sides of the fish, and press these into position. (There is no need to use water or egg white to secure the fins as the marzipan will be sufficiently sticky.) Allow the fish to firm up for about 1 hour, then use the tip of a teaspoon to make scales and gills in the marzipan (see photo 1).

6 Make up separate solutions of pale blue and pink colouring by mixing paste food colourings with water. Brush these over the fish (see photo 2), blending the colours together where they meet by simply dabbing lightly back-

wards and forwards until the colours merge. The colour will pick up the indentations scored in the marzipan. Do not worry if the colouring looks a bit rough at this stage. Allow to dry.

7 Using food colouring and lustre powders of similar, or perhaps contrasting, colours, brush the fish all over. This will not only cover up the original colour to some extent, but will also add a wonderful watery lustre. Silver lustre powder is very good for this.

8 When the fish is completely dry, place the pieces in position on the cake. Flatten two small balls of marzipan for the eyes, and fix in position with a dab of water or lightly beaten egg white. Colour a small amount of marzipan black, shape it into two very small, slightly flattened rounds, and fix one in the centre of each eye. Paint broken lines of dark blue food colouring on the surface of the cake around the head and tail of the fish to represent ripples on the water.

9 To make the bulrushes, paint six or eight wooden kebab skewers with green food colouring. Colour 250g (8oz) of the remaining marzipan a deep chestnut brown and roll it into six or eight sausage-shaped pieces. Push the skewers through the sausage-shaped pieces. Allow to dry for several hours.

10 To make the leaves to accompany the bulrushes, lay a length of florist's tape on a flat surface and moisten it lightly with a little water. Lay a piece of florist's wire down the centre of the length of tape, then lay another piece of tape on top. The two pieces of tape will stick together, fixing the wire in the centre. Using scissors, cut the tape into an elongated leaf shape and fix it to a bulrush, winding florist's tape

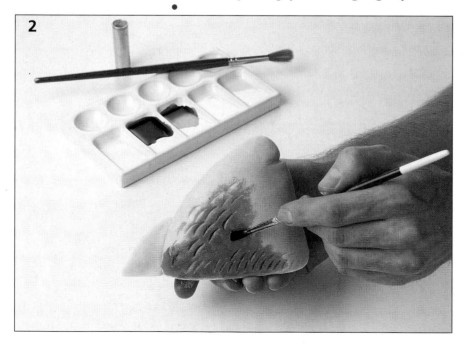

round to hold the stems together. Repeat to make as many leaves as you need.

11 To make the pebbles, colour the remaining marzipan with two or three different shades of blue, green and black. Knead the colours only lightly into the marzipan, stopping well short of completely amalgamating them, so that when you break off pieces and roll them into pebbles you will be left with a marbled effect (see photo 3).

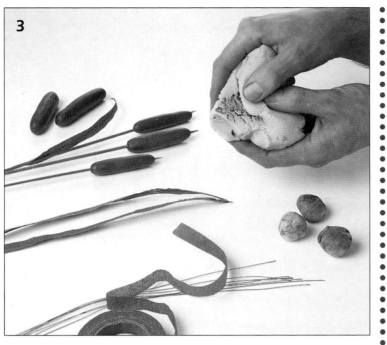

12 Arrange the pebbles on top of the cake and on the board around the base. Insert the bulrushes into the top of the cake, or into the pebbles around the base.

13 To make an entirely edible message for the cake, roll out the gelatin icing on a surface lightly dusted with cornflour, and cut out a piece measuring 15 x 2.5cm (6 x 1 inch). Cut out a second piece measuring 10 x 7.5cm (4 x 3 inches). Cut one end of the long piece and the two shorter sides of the larger piece into ragged shapes so they will look like broken off pieces of wood. Trace the message of your choice from page 91 on to greaseproof or non-stick paper, enlarge it as necessary (see page 10), then lay it over the larger piece of icing while it is still soft. Go over the message again with the end of a cocktail stick, pressing hard enough to leave the message imprinted in the icing. Leave it to harden for several hours.

14 Using paste food colourings diluted with water and an artist's

paintbrush, paint over the outline of the message on the icing, then paint the remaining icing with a brown wood grain effect (see page 17). Leave to dry, then stick the two pieces of icing together with a small amount of royal icing. Leave to dry.

15 For a message to keep rather than eat, allow the icing pieces to harden completely, then paint them with a wood grain effect. When the paint has dried, transfer the message to the icing using a sheet of carbon or graphite paper. Stick the two pieces together with royal icing and leave to dry. (Alternatively, if you prefer, the message can simply be made from a cut-out piece of card.)

16 Push the message board gently into the surface of the cake. For an amusing touch, wrap one of the fish's fins around the base of the placard so it looks as though the fish is holding it up out of the water.

Bulging Bicep

Oiled, sleek, lycra-clad and proud, modern man and woman are out there going for the burn, and pumping iron in pursuit of the body beautiful. Decorating that body with tattoos only seeks to emphasize those pendulous pectorals, fabulous forearms and bulging biceps, while at the same time providing a novel idea for including a message on a cake. Whether it be 'Who Dares Wins' or simply 'I Love My Mum', just change the message to suit the occasion!

YOU WILL NEED

one 30cm (12 inch) square cake (see pages 8–9)
one 36cm (14 inch) standard square cake board
apricot jam, sieved
1kg (2lb) marzipan
icing sugar for dusting
750g (1½lb) fondant icing (see page 13)
paste food colourings and dusting powders

EQUIPMENT

artist's paintbrush
cocktail sticks

1 Place the cake on the cake board. Trace the bulging bicep design on page 93 on to a piece of greaseproof or non-stick paper, and enlarge it so that it fits snugly within a 30cm (12 inch) square. Cut out the design and place it on top of the cake. Using a stiff-bladed knife, cut the cake around the paper template (see photo 1).

2 To shape the cake, cut off the edges and round them down to emphasize the curves of the muscles. Undercut the cake where it meets the board to make the arm more rounded. For an authentic shape, carve the 'forearm' part of the cake (from elbow to wrist) so that the

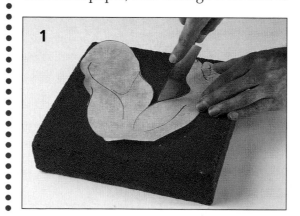

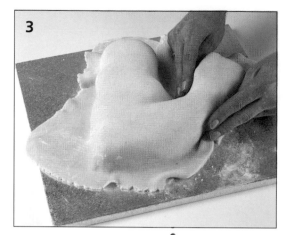

top curves upwards from the elbow to halfway down the fore-arm, then curves gently down to the wrist, and up again for the fist. Hold your arm against your side to see exactly how this should look (see photo 2).

3 Spread the cake all over with apricot jam. Roll out the marzipan on a work surface lightly dusted with icing sugar into a sheet large enough to cover the whole cake. Smooth the marzipan over the cake (see Cook's tip on page 50), tucking it in

well at the base (see photo 3), and trimming neatly around the edges.

4 Colour the fondant icing either a 'flesh' tone, golden brown or pink. Roll out the icing on a work surface lightly dusted with icing sugar and use it to cover the cake just as you covered it with marzipan, feeding a fold of icing between the bicep and fist. Smooth the icing all around, trim it neatly and allow it to dry overnight. Additional shading can be added by brushing food colour powder lightly on to the icing.

5 Trace the tattoo artwork on page 93 with an appropriate message on to a sheet of greaseproof or non-stick paper, and enlarge it in proportion to the cake (see page 10). Lay the design over the arm and gently score over the lines using the end of a cocktail stick, darning nee-dle or something similar to mark the out-line of the design on the icing. Remove the paper and paint in the design using a variety of paste food colourings (see photo 4). Paint 'crease' lines and finger-nails on the fist. Leave to dry.

The message this muscular creation carries is entirely up to you. Make up something that will mean some-thing special only to you and your partner, or 'bor-row' one of the messages on page 93.

Frog Prince

It is said that in order to find your prince, you have to kiss an awful lot of frogs! Lurking within that bug-eyed, green, slimy beast could be the man of your dreams! Whether he turns into a prince or not, this amusingly leering creature gives enormous opportunity to celebrate virtually any occasion. Although fairy-tale princesses were less likely to be turned into frogs than to drop into a dead faint at the prick of a pin or the taste of an apple, there is no reason why this cake shouldn't be given to a female friend or family member.

YOU WILL NEED

four 25cm (10 inch) square cakes (see pages 8–9)
one 36cm (14 inch) standard round or square
cake board
apricot jam, sieved
1.75kg (3½lb) marzipan
icing sugar for dusting
1.5kg (3lb) fondant icing (see page 13)
green, yellow, black and silver (optional) paste
food colourings
food colouring and lustre powders
250g (8oz/1 cup) gelatin icing,
see page 14 (optional)
cornflour for dusting

EQUIPMENT

artist's paintbrush
Christmas tree ornament (optional)
sweets or dragees (optional)
false jewels (optional)

1 Pile the cakes on top of each other to form a cube, and stand them on a 36cm (14 inch) round or square cake board. Turn the cube so that one corner of it is nearest to you. Place a long, sharp, rigid-bladed knife at an angle of about 45°, one third of the way in from one corner of the top cake (see photo 1). The point at which you start cutting

establishes the top of the frog's head, and the first cut you make will shape the back of its head and the curve of its back down to its bottom. Cut through the cake in a line sloping gently out and down, starting at the top and emerging about 5cm (2 inches) from the bottom opposite corner (see photo 2). Trim the cake to make it as smooth as possible.

2 Using the point of a knife, score two semi-circles in the sides of the cake (see photo 3) to form the tops of the frog's back legs. Begin these lines close to the frog's bottom, then extend them in a curve upwards to the height of two

Cook's tip

The success of this cake depends on carving. Although it might look a bit complicated, it is easier than it seems, and is lots of fun. Before you start, read all the instructions and look carefully at the photos, to give you a clear idea of how the shape develops from beginning to end. Also, remember that it is helpful to have something to copy, such as a child's toy frog, an ornament or an illustration in a book.

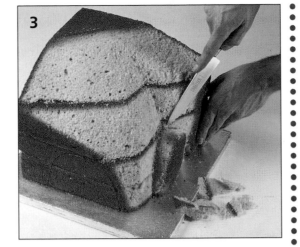

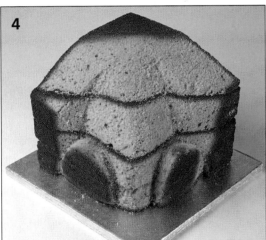

cakes, and then down to a point about 7.5cm (3 inches) short of the adjacent corner of the cake. Check that the scored outline is the same on both sides of the cake before you start carving. Once you are happy, cut 3.5cm (1½ inches) into the cake along these lines. To reveal the legs, carve out and down from the high point of the frog's backbone, until you meet up with the line that you have just carved into the sides. In this way you will be able to remove surplus cake and shape the sides of the frog and both its back legs (see photo 4). Be sure to stop at the line that establishes the top of the leg. If you cut beyond this, you will actually be cutting into the leg itself.

3 To carve the head, turn the cake around. The head is carved using the depth of the top two cakes (see photo 5). (If you think it might be a little difficult to carve out the eyes, you can simply add marzipan eyes later.) To carve the head, cut from the top of the head out and down towards the front corner, emerging at the front edge, cutting through the depth of the top cake only. Remove the excess cake. Continue to shape the head by cutting from the front of the head gently out and round to the sides. Clear away excess cake. Carve in a line down and in from the tip of the frog's nose to form the 'chin', cutting through the depth of the second layer of cake. Cut out and round to the sides to shape the bottom half of the head.

4 Before beginning to carve the front legs, take a look at photo 7. This gives the side view of the frog, and shows how the various parts of the body relate to each other. In particular, note that the front legs are carved using the bottom two layers of cake.

Starting on one side, form the back edge of the front leg by cutting a diagonal line, sloping from back to front of the frog. Cut into the side of the cake to a depth of 3.5cm (1½ inches), cutting down from the top of the second layer of cake towards a point on the board beneath the chin of the frog. When you have cut this line, gently carve away the cake between the back and front legs, thereby exposing the side of the frog. Repeat on the other side of the cake. The remaining part of the front legs and the chest are formed by cutting away a triangle of cake from under the frog's chin, reaching almost down to the board. Start carving under the chin and cut downwards and in to produce a slightly portly tummy, and to reveal the top of the front legs (see photo 6).

5 All the main features of the frog are now in place. Take a look at your frog and gently round down any corners or edges, refining any details you think need it. The marzipan can be applied to the cake in just three pieces. For the first piece, spread apricot jam on the back of the frog extending up to the top of its head and over its eyes, and down to its bottom, and around the sides to a point just in front of the back legs. Roll out 1kg (2lb) marzipan on a work surface lightly dusted with icing sugar and drape it over the cake. Gently smooth the marzipan on to the frog until it is fixed in position (see photo 8). Trim away excess marzipan, reserving the trimmings. Remember to keep the edges of the marzipan as tidy as possible as poor seams will show clearly underneath the fondant icing.

6 Spread apricot jam over the remaining cake, except the face. Gather up the marzipan trimmings and add a further 500g (1lb). Roll it into a rectangular piece and wrap it around the front and sides of the frog, pressing it into place and marrying up the seams as neatly as possible. Trim away excess marzipan, reserving the trimmings. Finally, roll out the remaining 250g (8oz) marzipan together with the trimmings. Spread the remaining cake with jam, and press the marzipan into position, joining the seams neatly. It is important to keep the head and face as neat and sharply defined as possible, so if you have any folds of marzipan or any irregularities, try to smooth them under the frog's chin where they can be hidden or disguised. Leave to firm up overnight.

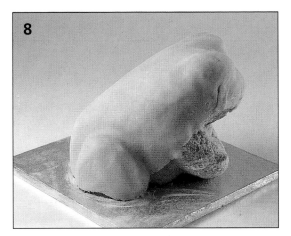

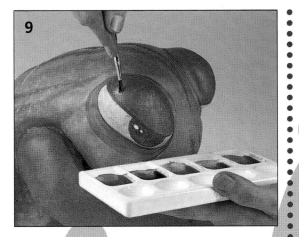

7 The cake is covered with three pieces of fondant icing in the same way as it is covered with marzipan. To give your frog a matt, uniform green colour, colour the fondant icing with green paste food colouring before rolling it out. However, for more variety, colour and character, cover the frog with white fondant and paint it afterwards (see step 8). To help the icing stick to the cake, brush the marzipan with boiled water. The back and sides will need 750g (1½ lb) fondant icing, the sides and front (not including the face) will need 500g (1lb) plus any trimmings remaining from the back, and the face will need 250g (8oz), plus any remaining trimmings. Make the seams as neat as possible; if there are any folds of icing when covering the head, try to press these under the chin where they will not be seen.

8 If you have covered your frog with green fondant icing, you can add more colours either by stippling over the base colour or by brushing on powder food colourings. If your frog is covered with white fondant, make up a series of shades of green and yellow in a palate (see photo 9). Begin by painting dark green lines around the eyes to outline them, and to emphasize the lids and folds of skin under the eyes. Paint on a smile. Stipple lines of dark green

down the back and sides and around the legs, to add detail (see page 18 for more information on stippling). Using the other colours in turn, stipple all over the surface of the icing, adding yellow and paler shades of green to create character and add emphasis. Finally, using black food colouring, add the eye balls. Leave the colouring to dry. Once the colouring is dry, further detail can be added by brushing the frog with lustre powders, or food colouring powders, making the skin look shiny and wet.

9 The final detail, the crown, is made from a Christmas tree ornament. A simpler version can be made from card or gelatin icing using the outline on page 93. Simply trace the outline on to greaseproof or non-stick paper, enlarge it to fit your frog (see page 10), transfer it to thin card and cut it out. Roll out the gelatin icing on a work surface lightly dusted with cornflour, lay the crown design on it and cut out the icing around it. Leave the icing for 1–2 minutes, then simply bend the two ends round and stick the edges together with a very little water. The icing will be firm enough for the crown to be left to dry standing up. If you wish, paint the crown in silver food colouring and decorate it with sweets or dragees (if you might like to eat it), or with sequins and false stones (if you won't).

If you'd like to add a message to your frog, make a gift tag or placard as described on pages 27 and 49. Your message could be: 'Make my day – kiss me' or 'I'm green, I'm slimy, I'm yours'.

My Heart Has Wings

When you can't sleep, look constantly distracted, and deep sighs punctuate the air, it's either time to call the doctor, or it's love! Floating inches off the ground, you could swear your heart had wings! Whether it's a brand new relationship or one that still leaves you feeling giddy after many years, why not let your loved one know with this wonderfully simple but expressive creation. This cake is equally effective whether made to celebrate an anniversary, an engagement, or simply a shared happy memory. You can change the message to suit the occasion.

YOU WILL NEED

one 25cm (10 inch) round cake (see pages 8–9)
one 30cm (12 inch) thin round cake board
apricot jam, sieved
500g (1lb) marzipan
icing sugar for dusting
1.5kg (3lb) fondant icing (see page 13)
one 36cm (14 inch) standard square cake board
pink, blue and mauve food colouring powders
red and blue paste food colouring
750g (1½lb/3 cups) gelatin icing (see page 14)
cornflour for dusting
royal icing (see page 13)

EQUIPMENT
artist's paintbrush
cocktail stick

Cook's tip

If you have, or can borrow or hire, a 25cm (10 inch) heart-shaped tin, then use this to bake the cake.

1 Trace the heart-shaped template on page 94 on to a piece of greaseproof or non-stick paper and enlarge it so it will fit neatly within a 25cm (10 inch) circle. Cut out the heart shape and lay it on top of the cake. Cut the cake away around the paper (see photo 1).

2 Using a sharp, rigid-bladed knife held at an angle of 45°, trim off about 2.5cm (1 inch) of the cake all around the edges (see photo 2). Continue to cut away the cake, trimming any remaining edges until the cake resembles a plump, heart-shaped cushion. Place the cake on a 30cm (12 inch) thin round cake board.

3 Spread the cake with apricot jam. Roll out the marzipan on a surface lightly dusted with icing sugar and use it to cover the cake (see page 16). Trim away the excess and leave to firm up.

4 Roll out 750g (1½lb) fondant icing on a surface lightly dusted with icing sugar and use it to cover a 36cm (14 inch) standard square cake board. Trim the fondant icing neatly at the edges of the board. Leave to dry for several hours or overnight.

5 Trace a variety of cloud shapes on to greaseproof or non-stick paper, using the templates on pages 94–95. Enlarge the shapes as necessary (see page 10), then transfer them to stiff paper or card using carbon or graphite paper, and cut them out. Put some pink, blue and mauve food colouring powder in separate mounds on a saucer. Hold one of the cloud outlines on the iced board and, using a dry artist's paintbrush or a stencil brush, dip it into one of the powder colours. Do not overload the brush, and be sure to tap off any excess. Gently dab the colouring along the edge of the cloud shape, and slightly above it (see photo 3). Reload your brush as necessary, using a variety of colours and blending them together on the board, so that a cloud might start off blue and then shade into mauve and then pink. Repeat the clouds as many times as you wish, moving the template over the iced board.

6 Colour the remaining fondant icing a lovely deep red. Roll it out and use it to cover the cake (see page 16), trimming it neatly around the base. Leave the icing to harden for several hours or overnight. To move the cake on to the cloud-covered board, gently bend the thin cake board downwards to free it from the icing around the base of the cake. Slide a palette knife under the cake and lift it carefully into the centre of the square board.

7 To make the message, roll out 250g (8oz/1 cup) gelatin icing on a surface lightly dusted with cornflour. Cut out a strip measuring about 36 x 5cm (14 x 2 inches) and lay it across the heart, allowing it to extend down the sides and on to the board. Trace the message on page 94 on to greaseproof or non-stick paper and enlarge it to fit the icing strip (see page 10). Place the paper over the fresh strip of icing and score over the message with the end of a cocktail stick, pressing hard enough to leave an impression in the soft icing. Leave to dry for several hours before painting the message on the icing in red.

8 To make the 'folds' of icing around the message, knead another 250g (8oz/1 cup) gelatin icing until it is soft and supple, and roll it out. Cut out two pieces, each measuring 36 x 10cm (14 x 4 inches), and shape them into loose folds. Arrange these folded strips above and below the message, being careful not to obscure it. (These additional strips of folded icing are not strictly necessary; the message can be left plain, if preferred. However, they are very effective and add a touch of romance to the cake. Leftover pieces of gelatin icing can be added to that used for making the wings.)

9 To make the wings, divide the remaining gelatin icing into three portions. Colour one portion a deep red, the second portion a deep pink, and the third portion blue. (Alternatively, the wings can be made from white icing and the colouring painted on afterwards.) Trace two large, two medium and two small wings on to greaseproof or non-stick paper using the outlines on page 94. Enlarge them in proportion to the cake (see page 10). Cut out the shapes, lay them on the icing, and cut away the icing around them, making two of each size and colour. Lay the wings together in two sets made up of one large, one medium and one small wing each, supporting the tips of the wings with crumpled tissue or kitchen paper (see photo 4). In this way, the wings dry with their tips tilted upwards, giving an impression of movement or flight.

10 If you have made the wings from coloured icing, simply finish them off by overbrushing the tips with colouring powders of different shades. If your wings are made from white icing, stipple various shades of colouring powders on to them as in the cloud background, merging them into one another on each wing. Leave the colour to dry.

11 Use a little royal icing to stick the wings together in sets and leave to dry. Gently push each wing into the icing covering the heart.

Medallion Man

Wherever you go, you will find him – at a wine bar, wedding reception or holiday disco, he lurks in the shadows waiting for his special moment. Suddenly it happens: 'Saturday Night Fever' hits the turntable and he takes centre-stage – Medallion Man! Everybody knows him – he's the chap who still thinks flares are fashionable, who insists on wearing his shirts unbuttoned to reveal a heaving manly paunch perfectly framed by a deeply ruffled shirt! To top it all, medallions jangling! The female equivalent wears her dresses too tight, revealing a VPL (visible panty line), and a bra two sizes too small. Instead of medallions, she sports clanking jewellery, possibly with her name spelt out in beads or twisted wire! If you have a style guru in your family, here is your chance to poke affectionate fun and tell him or her what even a best friend won't say.

Choose a message to suit, and dance the night away!

YOU WILL NEED

one 30cm (12 inch) square cake (see pages 8–9)
one 36cm (14 inch) standard square cake board
apricot jam, sieved
750g (1½lb) marzipan
icing sugar for dusting
1.5kg (3lb) fondant icing (see page 13)
'flesh', claret, black, rose pink and brown paste food colourings
250g (8oz/1 cup) gelatin icing (see page 14)
cornflour for dusting
royal icing (see page 13)

EQUIPMENT
artist's paintbrush
cocktail stick
icing shaping pad or 'bubble wrap'

1 Trace the Medallion Man outline on page 95 on to a sheet of greaseproof or non-stick paper, and enlarge it so that it fits neatly within a 30cm (12 inch) square (see page 10). Place the cake on a 36cm (14 inch) standard square cake board. Cut out the paper outline, lay it on the cake and cut away the cake around it (see photo 1).

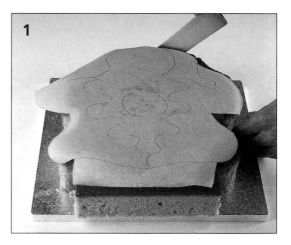

2

2 To carve the top of Medallion Man's trousers, score a line with the tip of a knife 3.5cm (1½ inches) in from the bottom edge of the cake, right across the surface. Following this line, cut down 1½ cm (¾ inch) into the cake. Now cut a line 1½cm (¾ inch) down from the top of the cake along the bottom side, cutting in until you meet the first cut. Remove the piece of cake cut off as a result. This leaves you with the top of the trousers where the belt will sit.

3 To shape the chest, cut a triangular shape in the centre of the cake to a depth of about 1cm (½ inch). The bottom of the triangle establishes the top curve of the tummy, while the two sides establish the outline of the somewhat saggy chest (see photo 2). Round down all angles, carving lines sloping out and down, being sure to emphasize those splendid 'love handles' and tummy hanging over the belt.

4 Spread the cake with apricot jam. Roll out the marzipan on a work surface lightly dusted with icing sugar, and drape it over the cake. Smooth the marzipan into position and trim it neatly at the base of the cake. With the tip of a

knife, hollow out a navel at the highest point of the tummy and gently round it off with a fingertip. Leave for several hours for the marzipan to firm up.

5 Colour 500g (1lb) fondant icing a pale 'flesh' colour. Roll out the icing on a work surface lightly dusted with icing sugar, and lay it over the cake. Smooth the icing into position and trim off any excess icing neatly at the base of the cake, reserving the trimmings. Colour 500g (1lb) of the remaining fondant icing an insistent shade, such as the wonderful plum (claret) used for the cake illustrated. Reserve 125g (4oz), roll out the remainder and cut it into two pieces. Arrange these at an angle over the pale flesh colour on either side of the torso, starting at the top of the belt and aiming for a point halfway between the neck and the shoulder on each side. Smooth into position and trim any excess icing neatly at the edges, reserving the trimmings.

6 Colour 250g (8oz) fondant icing grey using black paste food colouring. Roll out a sheet and place it over the bottom part of the cake, below the tummy. Smooth it into position and trim

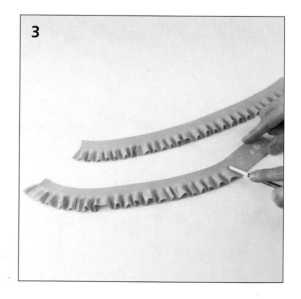

3

neatly to the edges. Add the trimmings of plum-coloured fondant to the 125g (4oz) reserved plum-coloured icing. Roll out a strip and mark a design on it with a shaping pad (see photo 4). (This pad leaves the impression of cobblestones, but is perfect for the belt. If you do not have a pad like this, you can use a piece of 'bubble wrap' instead. Simply place the 'bubble wrap' over the icing and gently roll a rolling pin over it. This gentle pressure should be enough to leave a pattern.) Place the belt in position and trim away any excess icing.

7 Combine the remaining 250g (8oz) fondant icing with the flesh-coloured trimmings, and colour it a contrasting shade to the shirt, such as the rose pink used for the cake illustrated. Roll out half the icing and cut it into four strips each 2.5cm (1 inch) wide and about 30cm (12 inches) long. Place the end of a paintbrush, knitting needle or something similar 1cm (½ inch) over the edge of the icing and press down on the edge, rolling the tool gently backwards and forwards until the icing 'frills' (see photo 3). When you have finished each one in turn, place it along the edge of the open shirt. You may need to attach

the frills by brushing a little water on the shirt. Trim each frill once in position and keep all the trimmings. Mark a row of dots with the tip of a cocktail stick down the length of the top frill on each side to represent stitching. Roll out the remaining rose pink icing, together with the trimmings. Trace the collar templates on page 95 on to greaseproof or non-stick paper, enlarge them, cut them out and use them to cut out the collar pieces. Fix in position with water.

8 To paint the chest hair, simply dilute some brown paste food colouring with a little water, and paint short dabbing strokes of colour on to the chest. (This can be omitted if you prefer.)

9 Roll out the gelatin icing on a work surface lightly dusted with cornflour. Trace the belt buckle and medallion templates on page 94 on to greaseproof or non-stick paper, including the lettering. Enlarge the outlines in proportion to the cake (see page 10). Cut out the shapes, lay them on the icing and cut the icing around them. While the icing is still fresh, score over the lettering using the end of a cocktail stick, pressing hard enough to leave an impression in the icing. Leave the icing to dry for several hours before painting in the details in your choice of colours. Fix the buckle and medallion in position with a little royal icing. The chain for the medallion can be painted on using dots of silver food colouring. Enhance the shape of the cake by painting on lines of pink food colouring to represent creases and shadows.

Ribbon Insert Wedding Cakes

A wedding should be a beautiful and memorable occasion, but, for those involved, planning one can be a nightmare, and even the most competent cake-decorator is likely to hand over the task of making the wedding cake to a 'professional'. With these cakes, however, even a relative novice is guaranteed to succeed with a simple technique that produces stunning results. It also has the added benefit of making a small cake look much bigger, so go on, cause a stir and turn a few heads – give them a cake such as they've never seen before.

RIBBON INSERT TECHNIQUES

Ribbon insertion work on more traditional cakes relies on the use of tiny ribbon that is difficult to see. In these cakes, we are aiming for flamboyance by using wider ribbon, and creating larger and more exaggerated loops. The principle is based on pushing folded ribbon into slits cut into the icing so that the ribbon appears to be threaded through the cake. In our cakes, the ribbon is in large part the basis for the decoration, so it is important that it should be beautiful in its own right. Perhaps even more important, though, is that it should be the type of ribbon that will hold a crease once folded. Some double satin ribbons are very soft and floppy and might not hold the larger loops without sagging.

1 Holding a ruler against the side of the cake, cut slits at regular intervals in the icing that are equal in length to the width of your ribbon. Use a sharp knife or scalpel so that the cuts in the icing will be as neat as possible (see photo 1).

2 Make creases in your ribbon at regular intervals, making sure you always crease the same side of the ribbon. If you are using a ribbon that is patterned on one side only, make sure you fold it so the patterned side will be on the outside. Cut a piece of thin but stiff card that is the same width as the

Cook's tip

It is a good idea to let your cake rest overnight after you have iced it and before you make any cuts in the icing. If you try to make cuts in the icing before it has had sufficient time to firm up, it might pull away from the side of the cake.

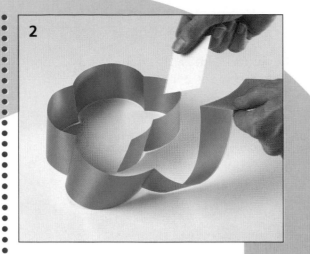

ribbon. This is used to help insert the ribbon into the slits in the icing (see photo 2).

3 Push the card neatly into a crease in the ribbon. Hold the crease against the slit in the icing and, using the card gently but firmly, push the ribbon into the slit. Once in position, gently pull the card out, leaving the ribbon in the slit. Continue by pushing the next crease into the next slit, and so on until you have moved all the way around the cake (see photo 3). The final loop will of course join up with the first. Tuck the remaining end of ribbon into the first/last slit in the icing. It should now be impossible to see where the loops begin and end.

4 The cuts in the icing can also be made horizontally up the sides of a cake, as well as vertically all around the sides. The process is exactly the same (see photo 4).

FOR THE THREE-TIER CAKE YOU WILL NEED

one 25cm (10 inch) round cake (see pages 8–9)
one 38cm (15inch) standard round cake board
one 20cm (8 inch) round cake (see pages 8–9)
one 25cm (10 inch) thin round cake board
one 15cm (6 inch) round cake (see pages 8–9)
one 20cm (8 inch) thin round cake board
apricot jam, sieved
2.25kg (4½lb) marzipan
icing sugar for dusting
1.75kg (3½lb) fondant icing (see page 13)
5 metres (5½ yards) ribbon

1 Place the largest cake on the 38cm (15 inch) standard round cake board. Place the middle-sized cake on the 25cm (10 inch) thin round cake board, and the small cake on the 20cm (8 inch) thin round cake board. Cover the cakes with marzipan and fondant icing in the traditional way (see page 16), allowing 1kg (2lb) marzipan and 750g (1½lb) fondant icing for the 25cm (10 inch) cake, 750g (1½lb) marzipan and 500g (1lb) fondant icing for the 20cm (8 inch) cake, and 500g (1lb) marzipan and 500g (1lb) fon-

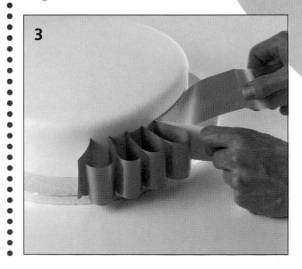

dant icing for the 15cm (6 inch) cake. Allow the icing to firm up overnight.

2 Remove the two smaller cakes from their cake boards by gently bending the board under each one downwards all around to loosen the icing and free the cake from the board. Place the middle-sized cake in position on the large cake. Place the smallest cake on top.

3 There are four main ribbon arrangements on this cake, each one running up the sides of the cake. You will need to use 1 metre (39 inches) ribbon for each of these. Instead of cutting slits in the icing, most of the ribbon creases are forced into the joins formed by the cakes sitting on top of another. The only horizontal cuts are made in the top of the top tier.

Although there are two different sizes of loop on this cake, the creases are made at exactly the same intervals down the length of the ribbon. If you look at the photo of the finished cake, you will see that the larger loops cascade down the depth of each cake, while for the smaller loops the ribbon turns back on itself and is forced into the same slit, thereby forming loops that appear smaller, although they do in fact use the same amount of ribbon.

At the top and bottom, the ends of each piece of ribbon are allowed to protrude from the slits, each one having a 'V' shape cut into it. The only other decoration is featured on the bottom tier, where two vertical slits are cut into the icing between each of the larger ribbon arrangements. Cut the remaining ribbon into four equal pieces, crease them in the same way, and tuck them into the vertical slits, allowing the 'V'-shaped ends to protrude.

Chosen for their delicate simplicity, gypsophila and forget-me-nots add a touch of romance to this cake.

VARIATIONS

Beautiful as it is, this delightfully simple cake becomes even more charming with the addition of elegant sprays of fresh flowers arranged on top and around the bottom tier.

The single-tier variation is made in exactly the same way, but can be finished off in a number of ways, most spectacularly when topped with a beautiful flower arrangement (see page 70).

You will see that, from this very simple technique, it is possible to make a huge number of variations simply by rearranging the sequence of loops or the positioning of the slits in the icing.

What could be simpler? This elegant cake is sophisticated in its purity – ideal for the couple who prefer a small celebration without any frills!

Stunning and dramatic, Casablanca lilies and deep red roses make the perfect wedding-day statement with passion!

'Do It Yourself!'

Some people can never take a hint! They will drive a car that looks like it has just crossed the Sahara, and never see the need to get out a bucket and sponge, or they will happily make a snack in a kitchen where ground-in dirt on the floor is begging to be given the once-over. Well, enough is enough – when all subtle hints have failed it's time to yell, 'Do it yourself'. These cakes are highly effective ways of getting the message across. Easier than they might seem, they promise an undoubtedly sweet revenge.

YOU WILL NEED

two 20cm (8 inch) round cakes (see pages 8–9)
750g (1½lb) marzipan
icing sugar for dusting
apricot jam, sieved
1kg (2lb) fondant icing (see page 13)
various paste food colourings
one 30cm (12 inch) standard round cake board
500g (1lb/2 cups) gelatin icing (see page 14)
cornflour for dusting
yellow or blue ribbon

EQUIPMENT

artist's paintbrush
carbon paper (optional)
DIY implements or cleaning equipment

1 To shape, cover and ice the cake 'bucket', follow the instructions given for making the pot in steps 1–3 of Cactus Willy (see pages 24–26), using 750g (1½lb) marzipan and 750g (1½lb) fondant. The only difference is in the colour of the fondant icing. A nice strong colour gives impact; a deep red has been used for the cake illustrated.

2 The effectiveness of this cake depends upon choosing suitable implements for moulding the decorations. Collect together a variety of items. For the DIY bucket, choose a hammer, paintbrush, screwdriver or spanner, modelling knife and saw; for the cleaning bucket, choose a scrubbing brush and plastic bottles of cleaning fluid (see photo 1). Make sure that they are all spotlessly clean. (It is assumed that decorations made in this way will not be eaten, but if you think they might be, then it is essential that the items used to mould them are thoroughly cleaned.) Roll out the gelatin icing on a work sur-

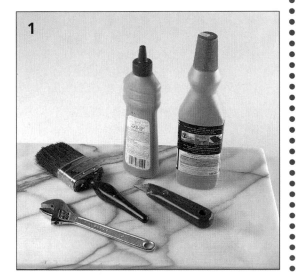

Cook's tip

The red colouring we have used for the fondant icing on this cake is a concentrated paste food colouring that develops a strong shade without making the icing too sticky to handle. It is very important to use paste colours in this particular instance as liquid colours would not work.

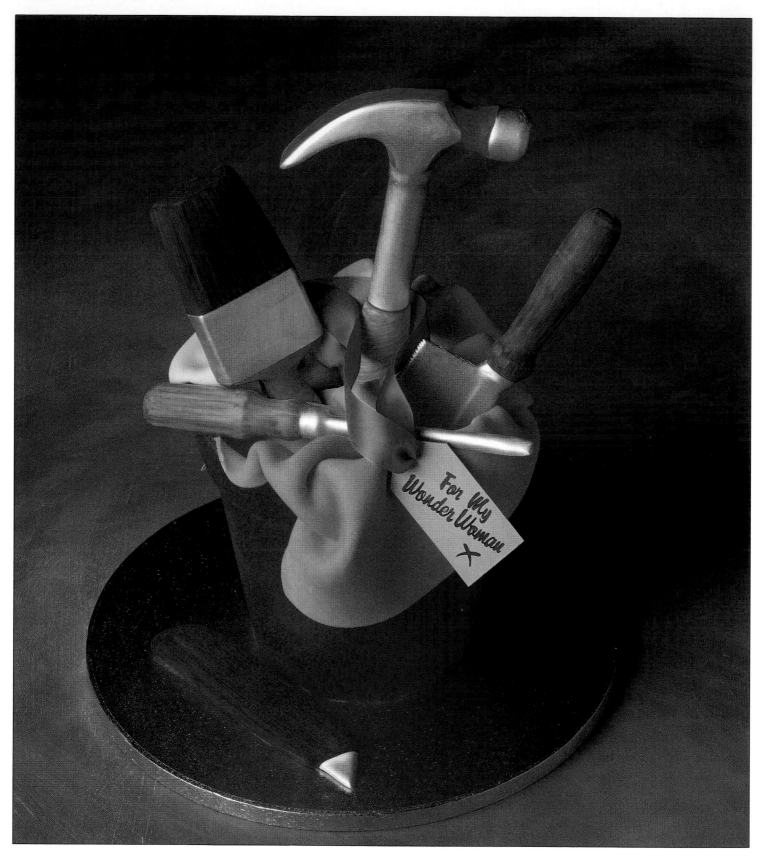

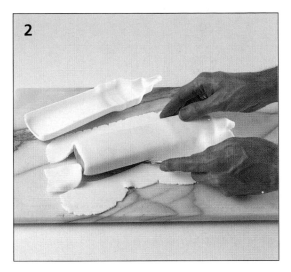

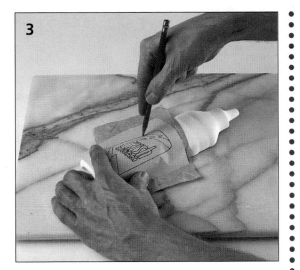

face lightly dusted with cornflour. Lay the icing over the various implements and gently mould it around the shapes underneath. Using a sharp knife or scalpel, carefully trim around each item in turn, making sure you give the items, particularly the bottles, some depth (see photo 2).

3 Allow the gelatin icing to dry in position for 4 hours. Remove the icing from the implements and turn each piece over to allow the underside to dry and harden.

4 Once the icing pieces are dry, make up a variety of colours by diluting paste food colouring with water, and use them to paint the icing pieces. The paintbrush, screwdriver, hammer and modelling knife are relatively simple, requiring only straightforward brushing on of colour. The bottles of cleaning fluid will take slightly more time as wording is involved. Trace the lettering on page 93 on to greaseproof or non-stick paper and enlarge it as necessary (see page 10). If the bottles are not to be eaten, then transfer the words directly on to the dry icing using carbon or graphite paper (see photo 3). (If the bottles are to be eaten, then lay the traced message over the icing while it is still

soft, and score over it with the end of a cocktail stick, pressing firmly enough to leave an impression in the icing. When the icing is dry, paint the message and finish off the bottle in bright colours.)

5 Roll out a small amount of gelatin icing and cut out a gift tag. Cut a hole in the tag for the ribbon. Trace the message of your choice from page 93 on to greaseproof or non-stick paper, enlarge it as necessary and transfer it on to dry icing using carbon or graphite paper, or score it into the soft icing as above. Paint the message in a nice strong colour.

6 To assemble the cake, gently push the icing decorations into the marzipan on the top of the cake. Divide the remaining 250g (8oz) fondant icing into two, and colour each piece a different colour. Roll out each piece in turn on a work surface lightly dusted with icing sugar, and drape them around the contents of the bucket, covering the surface of the cake. If you have any icing trimmings left over, you can also arrange a piece on the surface of the board, or make up a tablet of marbled soap. Finally, thread a piece of ribbon through the hole in the gift tag, and attach it to the cake.

Cook's tip

To save time, you can mould over just one side of each item. This will mean that the reverse side of each piece is hollow and can be left white. If you wish to make a complete bottle or paintbrush, for example, simply turn each item over and repeat the icing process. When the two halves of each item are dry, you can then fix them together with royal icing. Of course, this would take longer and require twice as much gelatin icing.

VARIATION

This cake provides plenty of opportunity for experimenting with different shapes and colour variations. You can also make it as personal as you like. If you use a particular brand of cleaning fluid in your bathroom, why not copy the colours and lettering from that? Use vivid colours as much as possible.

Fill your cake bucket with items that shout your message loud and clear.

Poppy Wedding Cake

There is something about the sight of a field of corn with poppies swaying in the breeze, set against a fabulous blue sky that can take your breath away. For this wedding cake, we have tried to incorporate all these elements of colour and fragility on a simple three-tier display, to produce something equally fabulous. There is nothing predictable about this particular centrepiece – it's a whimsical, joyous celebration to match your own!

YOU WILL NEED

one 25cm (10 inch) round cake (see pages 8–9)
one 38cm (15 inch) standard round cake board
one 20cm (8 inch) round cake (see pages 8–9)
one 25cm (10 inch) standard round cake board
one 15cm (6 inch) round cake (see pages 8–9)
one 20cm (8 inch) standard round cake board
1.75kg (3½lb) fondant icing (see page 13)
blue, red, yellow, green and black paste food colourings
apricot jam, sieved
2.25kg (4½lb) marzipan
icing sugar for dusting
750g (1½lb/3 cups) gelatin icing (see page 14)
cornflour for dusting
royal icing (see page 13)
wide green ribbon (optional)

EQUIPMENT

2 sets of four 7.5cm (3 inch) hollow silver wedding cake pillars
5mm (¼ inch) dowelling (see Cook's tip)
thin card
florist's paper or brown paper (see Cook's tip)
cocktail sticks
1cm (½ inch) plain cutter
heavy-gauge wire, such as coat-hanger wire
wire cutters
green florist's tape
fine wire

1 Put the 25cm (10 inch) cake on the 38cm (15 inch) board, the 20cm (8 inch) cake on the 25cm (10 inch) board, and the 15cm (6 inch) cake on the 20cm (8 inch) board. Colour the fondant icing sky blue and cover the cakes with marzipan and fondant icing in the traditional way (see page 16), allowing 1kg (2lb) marzipan and 750g (1½lb) fondant icing for the 25cm (10 inch) cake, 750g (1½lb) marzipan and 500g (1lb) fondant icing for the 20cm (8 inch) cake, and 500g (1lb) marzipan and 500g (1lb) fondant icing for the 15cm (6 inch) cake. Allow the icing to firm up overnight.

2 Arrange one set of wedding cake pillars on top of the largest cake. When you are happy with the arrangement of the pillars, gently but firmly press down on the top of each one to leave a faint outline of the base of each pillar in the icing. Remove the pillars. Repeat on the top of the middle-sized cake.

3 Pillars used on fondant-iced cakes are purely decorative; they do not bear the weight of the cakes. Instead, lengths of dowelling are inserted into the cake and the pillars used to disguise

Cook's tip

Dowelling is available from cake-decorating shops, usually in 20cm (8 inch) lengths. If necessary, however, you can buy untreated dowelling from any good hardware shop.

Cook's tip

The markings on the poppy petals are made with crumpled paper. Florists sometimes sell a type of paper that looks like rope and has to be unwound, producing paper that is full of wonderful creases and perfect for this task. Crumpled brown paper could also be used.

them. Use a ruler to measure the depth of the largest cake and the height of the cake pillars. Add these two measurements together and cut four pieces of dowelling to this length. Insert a length of dowelling into the very centre of each of the imprints made in the icing by the pillar bases. Push the dowelling straight down, holding it at right angles to the surface of the cake. Firmly tap the top of each piece of dowelling to ensure that it goes right through the cake and rests on the board beneath. Thread four of the pillars over the tops of the dowelling. Repeat on the middle tier, using four more pieces of dowelling and the second set of pillars. Leave the pillars in position to firm up for several hours before assembling the cake.

4 Using the template on page 91, trace the poppy outline on to greaseproof or non-stick paper. Enlarge it (see page 10) so it measures 15cm (6 inches) across, and use it to make a poppy template of thin card. Roll out 125g (4oz/½ cup) gelatin icing on a surface lightly dusted with cornflour. Lay the poppy template on the icing and cut out a poppy shape. Reserve the trimmings. While the icing is still soft, take a roll of crumpled paper (see Cook's tip) and, holding one end in the centre of the

poppy shape, roll the paper in a circle over all four petals (see photo 1). This will leave a fine tracing of lines resembling the veins on real poppy petals. Alternatively, simply score lines in the soft icing with the tip of a cocktail stick. For extra effect, roll the very edges of the petals with a small rolling pin or the end of a paintbrush to 'frill' them slightly (see Medallion Man's shirt, page 65). Place the cut-out petals in a small bowl to dry. For added detail, put small crumpled pieces of tissue or kitchen paper under some of the petals so that they dry in a more natural shape. Knead the trimmings together with another 125g (4oz/½ cup) gelatin icing, roll it out and use to make a second layer of petals. Allow one to dry immediately on top of the other so that they will fit perfectly together when hardened. Allow to dry for 4–6 hours. You need two layers of petals for each fully opened poppy. For the half-open poppies, leave the petals to dry in narrow glasses (see photo 2).

5 To make a seed pod, roll a small ball of gelatin icing into an oval. Flatten one end and, on the flattened top, score lines radiating out from the centre using a cocktail stick (see photo 3). Repeat, making one seed pod for each flower. To make a flower bud, roll a walnut-

Cook's tip
If you prefer to avoid too much painting, you can separate the gelatin icing into batches and colour it as required before rolling out or shaping it.

sized piece of icing into an oval. Score the fresh icing with a cocktail stick to represent a bud opening. With the end of the cocktail stick, lightly prick the outside of the bud all over to represent the tiny hairs that cover the buds of real poppies. Allow the seed pods and buds to dry on cocktail sticks. Finally, roll a little more gelatin icing into a thin sheet and cut out circles about 1cm (½ inch) in diameter, one for each flower.

6 When the petals are completely dry, paint them a brilliant poppy red or yellow. Allow to dry, and then stick the two layers of open petals together using a little royal icing. Paint a rough black triangle with feathered edges at the base of each petal. To colour the buds, paint the sepals green with a red strip between them on some, to make them resemble partially opened buds. Paint the seed pods green with thin black lines radiating from the centres of the flattened tops. Paint the small 1cm (½ inch) discs red. Allow all the pieces to dry completely.

7 The stamens used for the poppies can be bought from specialist cake-decorating shops. Use black stamens, if available, but if not, buy white stamens and colour them with black food colour-ing. If you can't find stamens, simply make small bunches of black thread or wool. To assemble the centres of the flowers, bend the stamens in half. Arrange them on top of each of the small red discs, radiating out from the centre, until you have a complete circle of stamens (see photo 3). Secure the sta-mens on the discs using a small amount of black royal icing. Fix a seed pod in the centre of the stamens on each disc with more black royal icing. Leave to dry, then fix one disc in the centre of each open flower with royal icing.

8 The flowers are supported on heavy-gauge wire. Note that at no time should this wire come into contact with the cake. Wrap a length of wire in green florist's tape and bend a loop in each end (see photo 4). Fix one loop to the cake board using stiff royal icing or glue. Bend the wire over the cake and attach the flower head to the loop at the other end of the wire using stiff royal icing. Repeat with as many flowers as you have. The buds are attached to thin-ner wire, also covered in florist's tape, and then taped on to the stems of the open flowers. Separate wind-blown petals can be added to the surface of the cake if you wish. Wrap green ribbon round the base of each cake, if liked.

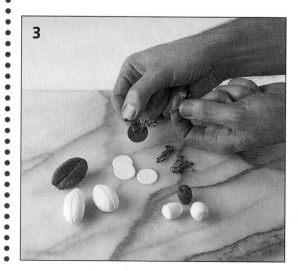

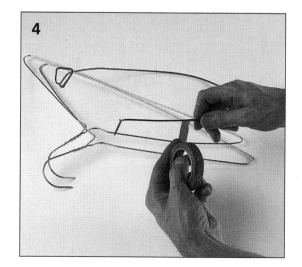

A Tartan Christmas

In a world of brilliant colour and design, one particular pattern stands out as a timeless classic – tartan. With its rich and varied application of colour, tartan enhances almost anything; in this wonderfully simple cake it is applied to icing. Whether for Christmas, New Year, or indeed any celebration, bring a touch of Scottish grandeur to your party!

YOU WILL NEED

one 25cm (10 inch) round cake (see pages 8–9)

one 38cm (15 inch) standard round cake board

apricot jam, sieved

750g (1½lb) marzipan

icing sugar for dusting

750g (1½lb) fondant icing (see page 13)

paste food colourings

750g (1½lb/3 cups) gelatin icing (see page 14)

cornflour for dusting

royal icing (see page 13)

EQUIPMENT

3.5cm (1½ inch) artist's sponge roller

artist's paintbrush

thin card

cocktail stick

20cm (8 inch) savarin mould

1 Place the cake on the cake board. Cover the cake with marzipan and fondant icing in the traditional way (see page 16). Leave the icing to dry overnight before applying the colour.

2 Mix two colours of your choice on one or two saucers or plates. The colours should be liquid but strong. If in doubt, try out the colour on paper before committing it to the icing. Roll a 3.5cm (1½ inch) sponge roller in one of the colours until it is coated but not wet.

To be sure, 'blot' the roller by rolling it gently backwards and forwards on the edge of the saucer or plate before applying it to the cake. Begin by rolling lines of colour across the top of the cake, pressing gently on the surface. (If you press too hard the colour might leak out of the roller in a pool.) You may need to roll over the same line several times to get a complete coating (see photo 1). The finish will be slightly textured because of the sponge. When you have completed a series of lines criss-crossing the top of the cake, roll up and down the sides to meet up with the ends of the lines on top. You will find that the roller cannot reach into the point where the cake meets the board; simply stipple

Cook's tip

The colours on the 'tartan' Christmas cake are applied using an artist's sponge roller. These rollers are available from art supply shops and are not expensive. However, a household paintbrush can be used instead if you cannot obtain a roller. The finish will be different, in that the colour will be flat rather than textured, but just as effective.

79

this area with a small artist's paintbrush loaded with the same colour to complete the design. Leave your first colour to dry for 15–20 minutes. Wash out your roller thoroughly and dry it. Repeat with your second colour, filling in the gaps on the cake. Allow to dry.

3 If you wish, you can add a third and contrasting colour. This is applied in thin lines across the cake and down the sides using an artist's paintbrush.

4 To make the poinsettias, trace the outline on page 95 on to greaseproof or non-stick paper, enlarge it so it measures 23cm (9 inches) across at its widest point (see page 10), and cut it out. Use the paper shape to make a thin card template. Roll out 125g (4oz/1 cup) gelatin icing on a work surface dusted with cornflour. Roll the icing out as thinly as possible so the flowers will be delicate. Lay the template on the icing and cut around it. Remove the template and score veins in the soft icing using a cocktail stick (see photo 2).

5 Place a 20cm (8 inch) savarin mould upside down on the work surface. Gently slide the petal shape to the edge of your work surface and on to your hand. (If you work carefully you can keep the whole shape intact.) Lay the icing petals over the mould, feeding the petals down into the mould so the centre of the flower rests on the work surface. Gently lift a number of petals and push small pieces of cotton wool or crumpled tissue underneath them so they dry supported (see photo 3). The remaining petals will dry following the curve of the mould. Gather up the icing trimmings and knead them with some more icing. Roll it out and repeat the process, laying the second layer of petals on top of the first and once again supporting several of them with cotton wool or tissue. It is important that the two layers of petals dry together so that they will fit perfectly together when dry. When dry, fix the layers together with a little royal icing. Repeat to make as many flowers as you wish. Allow the completed flowers to dry overnight.

6 To make the leaves, trace the outlines on page 95 on to greaseproof or non-stick paper, enlarge them in proportion

Cook's tip
Before laying the icing petals over the savarin mould, cut out a circle of stiff card that drops neatly into the hole. This way, if you want to move the mould off your work surface before the flower dries, the whole thing won't collapse and disappear through the hole when you lift it up.

Cook's tip

The flowers used to decorate the cake illustrated on page 80 are made from white icing and then painted with red food colouring once dry. If you prefer, you can mix concentrated red paste food colouring into the gelatin solution when making the gelatin icing (see page 14). This will produce a beautifully rich shade that is quite realistic when rolled out. This method of colouring the poinsettias also saves time. You would need to make 500g (1lb/ 2 cups) red gelatin icing.

to the flowers and cut them out. Use the shapes to make leaf templates of thin card. Colour some gelatin icing green and roll it out. Lay the leaf templates on it and cut out leaves. Score veins into the soft icing using a cocktail stick, then allow to dry for several hours. Once again, for a more natural look, lift some of the edges of the leaves and support them with cotton wool or tissue, so that they dry in a more natural curve.

7 To make the centres of the poinsettias, roll a small piece of gelatin icing into a ball the size of a large pea. Slightly flatten one end by pressing it on the work surface, and make the other end slightly pointed. Using a sharp knife or scalpel, cut a shallow cross in the flattened end. Repeat to make as many pieces as required – you might need as many as six or eight of these centres for each flower in order to ensure a more authentic poinsettia. Leave the pieces to dry completely, then paint the bottoms (the pointed ends) green and the tops yellow. When these two colours are dry, paint the indented crosses red.

8 To assemble the flowers, make sure that both sets of petals are stuck together firmly. Fix the centres into the poinsettias with a dab of royal icing and leave to dry. Place the complete flowers in position on the cake and arrange the leaves around them, fixing the whole lot in position with royal icing.

Shining christmas tree baubles and trailing ribbon make this into a cake full of the Christmas spirit – perhaps literally!

I Knew You Were Coming So I Baked A Cake!

How many times have you been in the kitchen, preparing something for guests about to arrive, and found yourself wishing that, like the Sorcerer's Apprentice, you could just snap your fingers and the meal would make itself, or the icing sugar would work its magic while you just put your feet up and watched? It's a nice thought, but sadly not one that is about to become a reality. This cake is possibly the nearest you will ever get to a cake that makes itself! It is deceptively simple, and the best thing about it is that it could be a cake for any occasion.

YOU WILL NEED

one 25cm (10 inch) round cake (see pages 8–9)
one 38cm (15 inch) standard round cake board
apricot jam, sieved
1.25kg (2½lb) marzipan
icing sugar for dusting
1.1kg (2¼lb) fondant icing (see page 13)
three 15cm (6 inch) round cakes (see pages 8–9)
750g (1½lb) royal icing (see page 13)
625g (1¼lb/2½cups) gelatin icing (see page 14)
cornflour for dusting
assorted paste food colourings
candles (optional)
wide ribbon

EQUIPMENT
20cm (8 inch) mixing bowl
artist's paintbrush

1 Put the 25cm (10 inch) cake on the 38cm (15 inch) standard cake board, and cover with marzipan and fondant icing in the traditional way (see page 16), using 750g (1½ lb) marzipan and 750g (1½ lb) fondant icing. Allow the icing to dry for 24 hours as it needs to be quite firm to take the weight of the remaining decoration.

2 Place the three 15cm (6 inch) round cakes on top of each other. Using a long, stiff-bladed knife, start cutting 5cm (2 inches) in from the edge of the

Cook's tip
Once you have assembled this fabulous cake, it is perhaps best not to try and move it any great distance. This is definitely a cake to make for a member of your own family or, if not, then be sure to invite the recipient to your place!

83

top of the top cake, and cut a long curving line out and down through the cakes, aiming for the blade to emerge just at the opposite edge of the bottom cake (see photo 1). For the second cut, place the knife 2.5cm (1 inch) in from the uncut edge of the top and cut down through the cake in a concave curve to emerge at the opposite uncut edge of the bottom cake. You have now carved the front and back edge of what will be the ingredients spilling out of the bowl.

3 To complete the 'spill' of ingredients, return the knife to the top of the cake and carve out and down all around the sides, always trying to emerge at the very bottom edge of the cake (see photo 2). When you have carved away the larger unwanted sections of the 'spill', take a smaller knife and finish shaping the cake by removing unwanted edges or irregularities. At this stage, it is worth pointing out that the mixing bowl made of icing will be supported on the top of this 'spill', so be sure to leave yourself something of a flat platform of cake at the top. This may look a little odd, but it will be disguised so don't worry unduly at this stage.

4 Spread the sides of the 'spill' with apricot jam. Roll out 500g (1lb) marzipan, plus any trimmings left over from covering the base cake, on a work surface dusted with icing sugar into a sheet large enough to wrap around the cake. Lift the marzipan on to a rolling pin and drape it around the 'spill', gathering any excess at the back, that is down the concave side of the 'spill'. Trim the marzipan neatly around the cake. Do not worry if the seams at the back, or the 'platform' at the top of the 'spill' appear untidy. All of the 'spill' will be covered and any irregularities will be hidden. Leave the marzipan to dry overnight. Keep any leftover marzipan. Lift the 'spill' carefully into position on top of the base cake.

5 Make up the royal icing, aiming for a consistency that is easily spreadable but stiff enough to hold its shape and not run once in position. Spread the icing over the 'spill' (see photo 3), remembering that the effect you are trying to achieve is of ingredients flowing

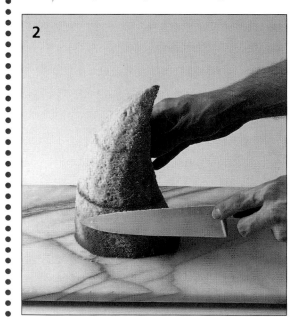

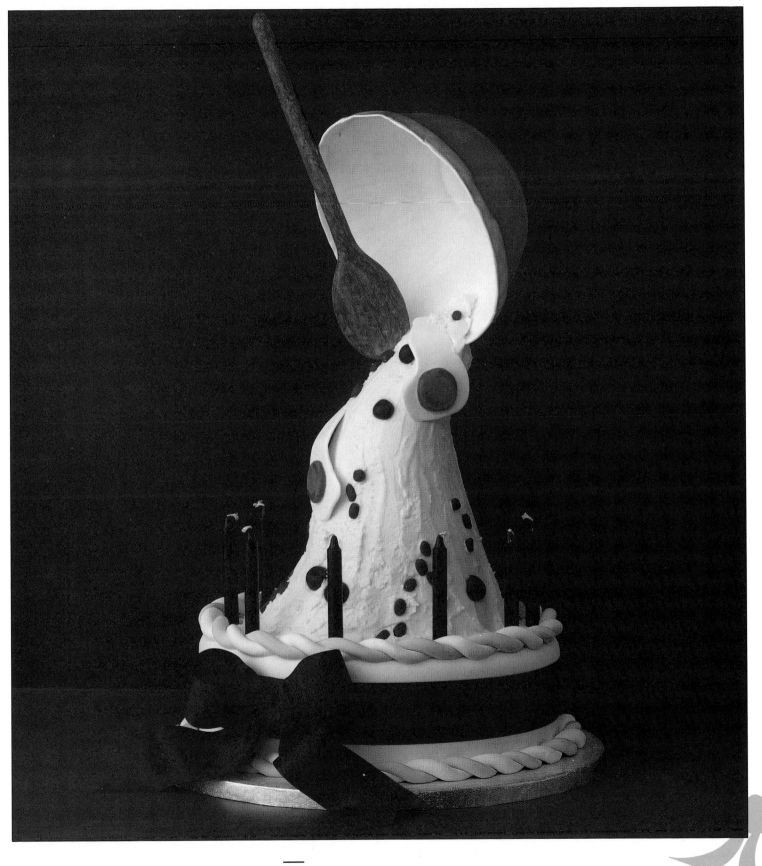

out of the bowl. Keep all spreading strokes vertical and as smooth as possible. Keep back some of the icing, if possible; if not, make up a little more to stick items on to the cake when putting it together. Allow the icing to dry completely for several hours or overnight.

6 The icing mixing bowl on top of the cake is made by covering a bowl with gelatin icing. The bowl we used measured 20cm (8 inches) across the top. If you prefer, it is possible to use a smaller bowl without losing any of the dramatic effect of the cake. Knead 500g (1lb/2 cups) gelatin icing until it is soft and pliable. Roll it out on a work surface lightly dusted with cornflour, and drape the sheet of icing over the upturned bowl. Using hands dusted with cornflour, gently but firmly smooth the icing over the bowl (see photo 4). If the icing is soft you should be able to stretch any creases out, so that you are left with an icing bowl without folds or cracks. If folds develop that you cannot get rid of, try to concen-

trate them in one area as it is possible to hide them when assembling the cake (see Cook's tip). Trim the icing to the edge of the bowl, reserving any leftover pieces and kneading them back into the remaining gelatin icing. Allow the icing to dry overnight before removing it from the bowl. Let the inside of the icing bowl dry for several hours. Once completely dry, paint or sponge the outside of the bowl with the characteristic golden brown colouring. When completely dry, the icing bowl we used for the cake illustrated weighed just 250g (8oz), so there is no need to worry about there being a large ungainly weight perched on top of the cake.

7 Roll out the remaining gelatin icing, and use some of it to cover a wooden or large metal spoon. Trim the excess icing neatly to the edge of the spoon and leave to dry. Cut out two egg whites and two egg yolks from the remaining gelatin icing, and allow them to dry supported over a rolling pin (or something similar) in order to give them an interesting shape. Remember to fix the 'yolks' on to the 'whites' with a little dab of water so that they dry in position together. When dry, paint the spoon in wood grain effect (see page 17) or silver. Paint the yolks a lovely egg yellow. To make the cherries and sultanas, colour some of the leftover marzipan Christmas red, and the remainder a mixture of brown and egg yellow. Roll small pieces of the red into balls, and the golden brown into irregular shapes. Allow to dry for about 2 hours on a sheet of greaseproof or non-stick paper. To finish off the cherries, make a dimple in the top of each one using the end of a paintbrush.

8 To assemble the cake, you will need more royal icing. However, it should be stiffer than the icing used to cover

4

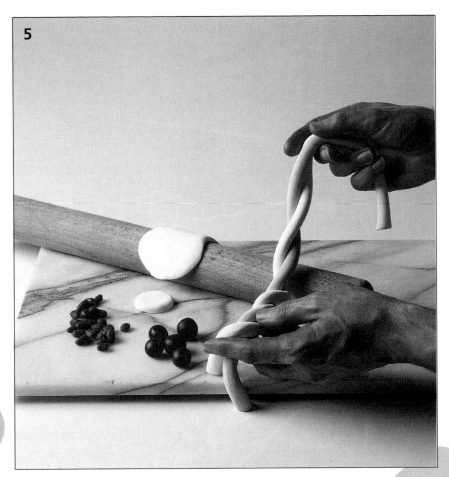

5

because you have to hold the spoon in position until the icing has firmed up. If you prefer, you can balance the spoon on the outside edge of the bowl, where gravity will hold it in place for you. Colour half the remaining fondant icing blue and roll it into a long 'rope' of icing on a work surface lightly dusted with icing sugar. Roll the remaining white icing into a similar 'rope' and twist the two together (see photo 5). On a cake of this size it is better not to try to make the rope in one piece. It will need to be quite long, and you might find that it will stretch as you twist it, resulting in a rope of uneven thickness that could crack. It is better, therefore, to make the rope in two halves, and to ask someone to help you lift them on to the cake.

10 Make more pieces of rope to go around the base of the cake. There is no need to stick the rope in place as fondant icing will stick to itself given time. Place the candles (if using) on the top of the cake, and tie a ribbon around the side. It is easier to tie a bow separately and then to fix it into position with royal icing later. Doing it this way also allows you to spend extra time on it and invariably produces a bigger and better bow.

the 'spill', as it must support the bowl. Apply liberal amounts of stiff royal icing to the top of the 'spill' and fix the bowl in position. Be sure to press the bowl firmly into position to ensure a good grip. Spread more royal icing inside the bowl and spilling out over the edge to give a more authentic look, as if the ingredients were really spilling out from inside the bowl. This extra icing will also help hold the bowl in position. Be sure to 'marry up' the newly applied royal icing with that already on the cake.

9 Fix the cherries, sultanas and eggs in position with a little royal icing. For the cake illustrated, we fixed the spoon as though it was helping scrape the mixture out of the bowl. This is undoubtedly magical but also a little precarious

Cook's tip

Fixing the bowl in position is simple but undoubtedly a bit nerve-wracking. To make doubly sure that it will stay put, you can add gum tragacanth to your royal icing, which will ensure that it sets very hard, or you could push two lengths of dowelling at an angle through the 'spill' and into the base cake, leaving 2.5cm (1 inch) protruding from the top. This will provide support for the back of the bowl while the icing sets around it. Of course, the dowelling rods would need to be covered so that they could not be seen.
If there are seams or cracks in your icing bowl, make sure that the bowl is fixed on top of the 'spill' so that they are covered up with royal icing.

Templates

Cadillac
(cake board)

Cadillac
(variation)

C

B

A

Cadillac

Just Married

U 2 R 1

Cadillac

C

B

A

BITTERSWEET

Cappuccino Kisses (variation)

Cadillac (variation)

Cappuccino Kisses

Cadillac

Cadillac (hotel)

90

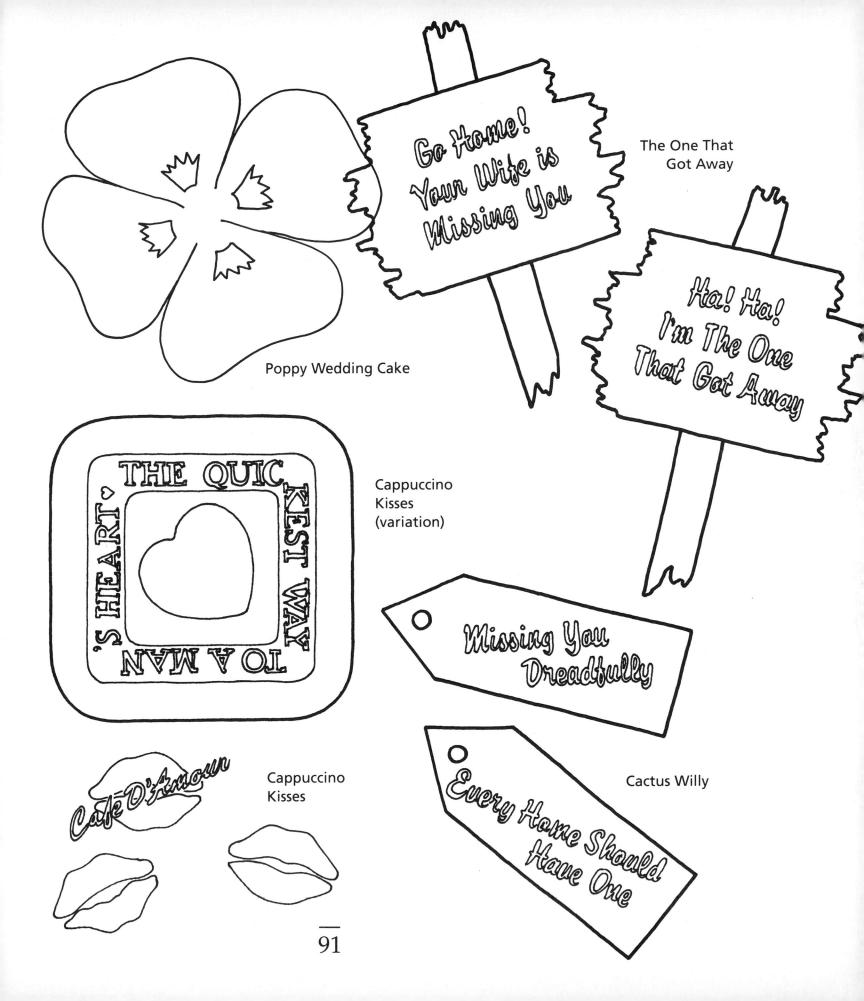

Poppy Wedding Cake

Go Home! Your Wife is Missing You

The One That Got Away

Ha! Ha! I'm The One That Got Away

THE QUIC KEST WAY TO A MAN 'S HEART

Cappuccino Kisses (variation)

Missing You Dreadfully

Cactus Willy

Café D'Amour

Cappuccino Kisses

Every Home Should Have One

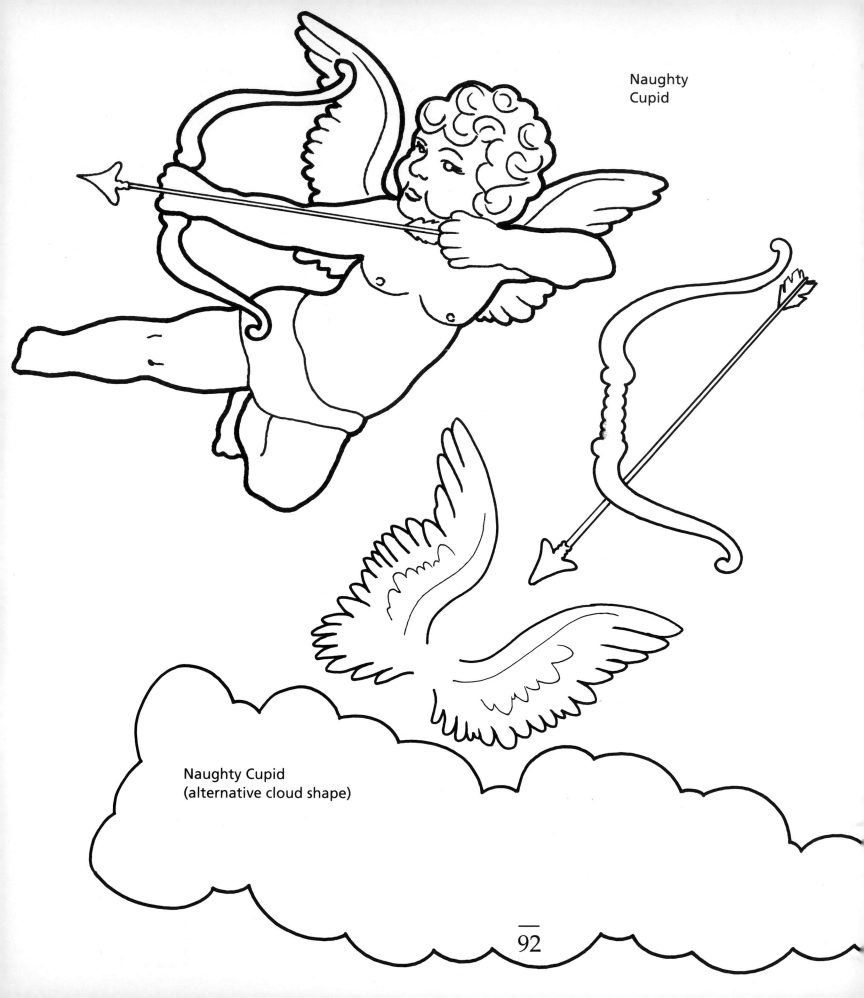

Naughty
Cupid

Naughty Cupid
(alternative cloud shape)

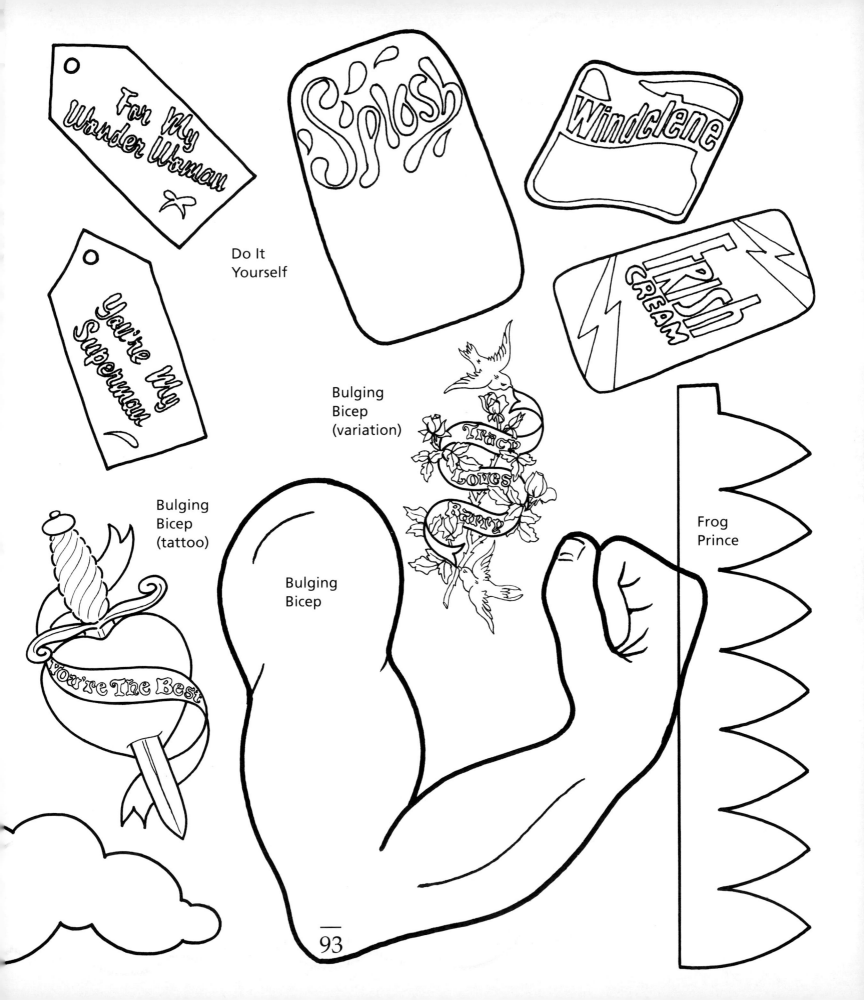

For My
Wonder Woman

Splash

Windclene

Do It
Yourself

IRISH
CREAM

You're My
Superman

Bulging
Bicep
(variation)

Tracy
Loves
Barry

Bulging
Bicep
(tattoo)

Frog
Prince

You're The Best

Bulging
Bicep

Medallion
Man
(buckle)

DELUXE

GROOVY
GUY
GROOVY

Medallion
Man
(medallion)

My Heart
Has Wings

My Heart Has Wings

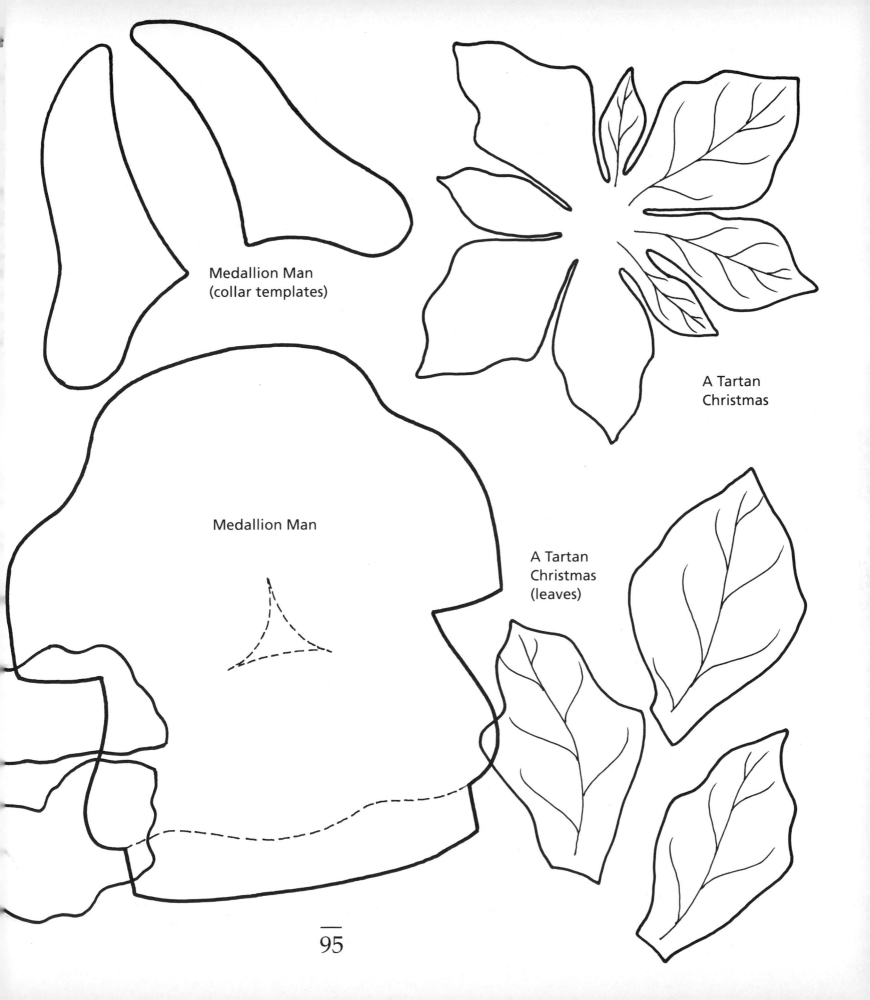

Medallion Man
(collar templates)

A Tartan
Christmas

Medallion Man

A Tartan
Christmas
(leaves)

Index